otl aicher

analogous and digital

with an introduction
by wilhelm vossenkuhl

published in co-operation with the
otl aicher archives

library of congress card no.:
applied for

british library cataloguing-in-publication data
a catalogue record for this book is available from the british library.

bibliographic information published by
the deutsche nationalbibliothek
the deutsche nationalbibliothek lists this publication in the deutsche nationalbibliografie; detailed bibliographic data are available on the internet at <http://dnb.d-nb.de>.

© 2015 wilhelm ernst & sohn, verlag für architektur und technische wissenschaften gmbH &, co. kg, rotherstraße 21, 10245 berlin, germany
© 1994 by inge aicher-scholl, 2014 by florian aicher

first published as *analog und digital* german edition
© 1991 by otl aicher, 1992 by inge aicher-scholl, 2014 by florian aicher

all rights reserved (including those of translation into other languages). no part of this book may be reproduced in any form – by photoprinting, microfilm, or any other means – nor transmitted or translated into a machine language without written permission from the publishers. registered names, trademarks, etc. used in this book, even when not specifically marked as such, are not to be considered unprotected by law.

translation: michael robinson
translation of the amended preface: übersetzungen hanns schiefele, bad reichenhall, germany

typesetting: thomson digital, noida, india
printing and binding: cpi ebner & spiegel, ulm, germany

printed in the federal republic of germany.
printed on acid-free paper.

2. edition

print isbn: 978-3-433-03119-3
epdf isbn: 978-3-433-60594-3
epub isbn: 978-3-433-60593-6
emobi isbn: 978-3-433-60590-5
obook isbn: 978-3-433-60596-7

contents

- 9   preface by sir norman foster
- 10   introduction
- 22   grasping with the hand and mind
- 28   extensions of the ego
- 36   the eye, visual thinking
- 47   analogous and digital
- 55   universals and capitals
- 60   buridan and peirce
- 63   reading scores
- 65   honourable burial for descartes
- 75   design and philosophy
- 93   architecture and epistemology
- 109   use as philosophy
- 133   planning and control
- 146   development, a concept
- 150   an apple
- 154   something quite ordinary
- 170   life form and ideology
- 178   cultures of thinking
- 188   afterword
- 190   sources

Otl Aicher was a good friend, mentor and working colleague. There was never a division between conversations on our work or any other subject - the topics ranged far and wide. Often as he was talking, Otl would pick up a piece of paper and illustrate his point with careful strokes of a ball-point. The combination was uniquely personal – witty, incisive and often thought-provoking.

During his summer retreats in August at Rotis, Otl would commit his thoughts to paper and these later became the subject of two books. Before then some of them had appeared randomly as articles in magazines or in editions. I remember being frustrated because I could not read German, even though I might guess at their content from the many hours spent with Otl hearing their story lines. I was also upset because I so much wanted to share Otl's insights with others around me; he seemed to be able to say with clarity and eloquence many of the things I felt needed to be said – as well as some of the things which we did not agree about. In his last years Otl was, I felt, at the height of his creativity in many fields, which ranged from visual communication and new typefaces to political and philosophical comment.

Following the tragedy of Otl's death I felt compelled to help make it possible for all of his writings to be translated and published in English. Otl saw through the stupidities of fashion and vanity. His opinions were so relevant to the issues of today that I believed it was important for them to be shared with a wider English-speaking audience – relevant to my own generation as well as students, professionals and the lay public.

Otl wrote rather in the way that he spoke and after some debate with those who were closer to him and who were also German speakers it was decided to leave the translation in its conversational form. We also felt that it was important to respect Otl's passionate objection to capital letters for starting sentences of marking traditionally important words. Perhaps it underlined his scorn for the pompous.

There was an integrity about the way that Otl lived, practised and preached. He would probably have been uncomfortable with the word preach, but I use it here in its most honourable and inspiring sense.

Norman Foster
London, January 1994

Introduction

by Wilhelm Vossenkuhl

Authenticity and a questionable analogy

"How is it", asks Edward Young, "that we are born as originals and die as copies?" The 18th-century English poet is concerned that as individuals in society we lose our distinctive qualities. We conform to other people, the taste of the times, but also to law and political order. Ultimately we do not know who we are and what makes us different from all the rest.

This concern about our authenticity has not got any less today. Authenticity is one of the great themes of Modernism. Young's contemporary Rousseau believes that it is only meaningful for us to exist in "unity of life with itself", in unity with nature. He suggests a new legal system to rescue authenticity, intended to create a community of life instead of abstract legal conditions.

It is hard for us to imagine today how we can do justice to the ideal of unity with nature in a bourgeois life community. And yet this ideal still seems fascinating. We have not stopped striving for it. But in our ecological epoch it means something different from what it did at the time of Rousseau.

Today we want to achieve unity with ourselves by the shortest possible route, and find our authentic selves without a detour via society. We strive for a direct, concrete relationship with our own nature and our natural environment. Society and its order seem to depend on the right relationship of the individual with nature, and not vice versa. A wareness of ecological dangers puts the natural before the social environment. The long-accepted precedence of society over the individual, at least from a political and legal point of view, has been questioned for quite some time. A new individualism with many pros and cons has prevailed for quite a while, at least in Western society.

Rousseau's suggestion appeared to be highly abstract to Lionel Trilling half a century ago. Trilling thought that our feeling for authenticity had become rougher, more concrete and more extreme (*Das Ende der Aufrichtigkeit*, Frankfurt/Main 1983, S. 92). When Trilling put forward this thesis in his lectures at

Harvard University it was easy to understand. However, his scepticism towards Rousseau at the time is now difficult to comprehend. On the other hand, the joy that Rousseau described as philosophical life in his "Rêveries" is accessible again (Heinrich Meier, *Über das Glück des philosophischen Lebens. Reflexionen zu Rousseaus Rêveries*, Munich 2011).

Striving to achieve unity with nature and an authentic self that is happy at the same time has come under pressure of time because of ecological dangers. It is no wonder that this pressure of time is making us increasingly impatient. This impatience increases our intolerance of the actual or presumed - agents of these dangers. But this impatience is a symptom in itself, not just a crisis of understanding ourselves and our unity with nature.

This crisis is not merely older than the ecological one. People like Rousseau, who were asking about our authenticity at the time of the Enlightenment, were already aware of it. But the attempt to solve this crisis leads in the wrong direction. In the late 18th century -after a long period of preparation through anatomy and early biological research - the thought that what was organic was natural became accepted.

It is not obvious at first how erroneous this thought is in terms of our self-perception and our relationship with nature. This is perhaps why it has lost none of its influence, even today. We come across it in criticism of modern technology and of literature. What makes this thought so plausible?

An organ is a complete entity, even if it is part of a greater whole, along with other organs; it plays a distinctive and irreplaceable role. It is difficult to find a more vivid image of authenticity than that of the organ. It conveys the thought that something authentic must have grown, it cannot be manufactured artificially.

The first critics of the age of the machine in the early 19th century, Carlyle and Ruskin, draw an analogy between the authentic and the organic. They see man's authenticity endangered by the mechanical principle of the machine. In their eyes everything that man creates for himself with technical aids is manufactured artificially, and therefore not authentic. Art, they think, along with 19th and 20th century Romantics, must also look to the organic if it wants to create something authentic. By the way, anyone who thinks that Carlyles and Riskins scepticism about the machine world was a long time ago and is long since obsolete is mistaken. Just recently we witnessed criticism of the machine and science era that was no less vehement in Michael Oakeshotts diaries (Michael Oakeshott, *Notebooks 1922-1986*, ed. by Luke O'Sullivan, Exeter 2014). Oakeshott also indirectly dealt with the analogy between the authentic and the organic in the form of what constitutes our integral nature as people, which is concealed from nothing and nobody. He spoke of the "terrorism of science" and turned against the superficial progress thinking that changes our nature. Like Ruskin, he believed that the commercialisation of life, industrialisation and money is the curse of our age. He claimed that this all deflects us from our actual selves. The question about the analogy between the authentic and the organic has obviously not gone away. But what is questionable about this analogy?

The thing that is questionable about the analogy is that it leads us astray due to a little metamorphosis. Because the organic inadvertently loses its meaning. The analogy, the image of the authentic, suddenly becomes a model, a kind of ideal. It appears as abstract as Rousseau's ideal of unity with nature in Trillings eyes. However, Rousseau's ideal is anything but abstract, because it is associated with the idea of freedom. Rousseau's message is that man can determine himself. Freedom is an active principle that guides the search for unity with nature in society. Man shapes his own identity.

The organic is not a model for active self-determination. It is more likely to condemn people to passivity and determination from outside. We do not even know what we are supposed to do when we orientate ourselves towards that which is organic, apart from shopping in health food shops, of course. The analogy between authentic and organic is questionable because it suggests that we can discover our own authenticity in the organic structure of the natural environment. However, our nature and our unity with the natural environment are determined and designed by ourselves, if at all. For this reason we are also responsible for our own nature and the environment.

Knowing and making

Self-determination and shaping nature remain abstract goals for as long as we do not know how we can realize them. What kind of knowledge do we need to determine ourselves? There are two kinds of knowledge to be dealt with here. One is knowledge of a plan that prescribes how the goal of self-determination can be reached. The other is knowledge that only develops in the course of concrete self-determination. We call the former theoretical and the latter practical knowledge. In one case the goal is fixed, in the other the goal only becomes concrete on the way to it.

Aristotle was already aware of both these kinds of knowledge. But two things were alien to him, the idea of self-determination and the idea that man can manufacture, can make himself. For this reason it does not make sense to transfer his views of theoretical and practical knowledge to the specifically modern idea of self-determination. We have to see how theoretical and practical knowledge were understood at the time of early Modernism, when the idea of self-determination came into being.

Modern understanding of theoretical knowledge was forged by Descartes in particular, and that of practical knowledge by Vico. For Descartes, determination of one's own self needed no experience. For him the ego has no history. It is a substance outside time and space, that we cannot doubt. Whenever I am in doubt about something I know that it is I who am in doubt. Descartes argues that this ego must be beyond doubt. Its theoretical features, like mathematical laws, simply have to be recognized, not newly discovered. For this reason there can be no problem of self-determination for Descartes. The ego is always the indubitable basis of all knowledge.

Vico, the counterpart of Descartes, believes that self-knowledge is historical. He sees in the "modifications of our own human mind" the principles by which we make history. Knowledge of history, and this is his fundamental thought, is formed in and through the making of history. We acquire practical knowledge by our own making, the manufacture of history.

Descartes' view of theoretical knowledge shaped the development of modern science, whose knowledge requires mathematics. With the aid of mathematics it has been able to and still can successfully formulate natural laws on the basis of experiment and hypothesis. Descartes formulated modern criteria of truth and the certainty of knowledge.

Vico's view of practical knowledge acquired through human making was denied this kind of success. This is partly because his view of making is inconsistent. It is true that we make history, but we, as God's creatures, follow the natural laws that he lays down. The idea of human self-determination is still alien to Vico.

Now which view of knowledge tells us that we are capable of selfdetermination? Apparently neither. Descartes sees no problem in self-determination, because in his understanding it is the basis of theoretical knowledge. Vico certainly introduces the thought of historical making, but he does not apply it to human self-determination because it was not yet a problem for him.

It is hardly surprising that these early modern concepts of knowing and making do not show which kind of knowledge we require to determine ourselves. The idea of self-determination, which is the basis of the search for authenticity and unity with nature, is unknown to early Modernism. And yet the two concepts identify the alternative types of knowledge that come into question as far as self-determination is concerned.

But a characteristic feature of Modernism is the fact that theoretical knowledge is considered superior to practical knowledge. The practical knowledge that is learned in historical making attracts little attention. Marx certainly takes up Vico's idea in *Das Kapital*, but does not apply it to man's relationship with nature. He believes in the emancipating power of technology. Marx, as Habermas critically points out, is thus involved in an ideology, that of belief in technology. This ideology is no better than its counterpart, hostility to technology.

However, in his early writings, the *Pariser Manuskripte* dating from 1844, Marx does develop a new concept of practical knowledge, that of self-manufacture through work. He sees work as a process of naturalization for man and humanization of nature. But this process founders if man sells his work for an abstract financial value. In doing this he alienates himself from his products, from work, and finally from himself.

Marx recognizes the mutual dependence between self-determination and making, between self-manufacture and work. He does not pursue this insight any more deeply than to provide a sketch of the stages of alienation. But his concept of alienation draws to our attention that we cannot determine ourselves if we

disregard that mutual dependence. We can either determine ourselves, or fail in the manufacture of things, in making.
Alienation is the opposite of authenticity. We can either determine ourselves in making, or we fail, and put ourselves in danger. Making is clearly ambiguous, just as ambiguous as technology. Today we no longer speak of alienation, but of the way we are endangering and destroying ourselves, the natural environment and our culture. What kind of making would not put us in danger, but allow us to determine ourselves?

Thinking and making

In this collection of essays, Otl Aicher attempts to answer this question. He develops a philosophy of making that works from the basic thought that thinking and making are so interdependent that one can be understood only in terms of the other. Aicher demonstrates that up to now we have misunderstood the making and therefore have a one-sided opinion of thinking.

He reproaches us to neglect the practical side of things compared to their theoretical side. For this reason we overestimate the importance of what Otl Aicher calls "digital": abstract conceptuality and logical precision. But we underestimate the visual, things that are learned from practical experience and sensual perception, which Aicher calls "analogous". But Aicher is convinced that the abstract and digital can no more be separated from the concrete and analogous than conceptual thinking from our sensuality. Mental and physical making are related to each other and dependent upon each other. If we disregard this mutual relationship we endanger ourselves and our world.

Without any obligation towards philosophical tradition and without taking any particular model, Aicher adopts the concept of practical knowledge that is touched upon by Vico and Marx. He gives a new meaning to this concept. It is intended to overcome the split in modern consciousness, the division between abstract and concrete thinking, between digital and analogous. He does not try to find a counter-concept to theoretical knowledge, but criticizes its one-sidedness. He wants to show that this one-sidedness is partially responsible for the crisis of rationality and our self-perception in Modernism.

Aicher is convinced that the concrete comes before the abstract, *anschauung* before reason, truth before knowledge. He finds sufficient justification for this in Ockham, Kant and Wittgenstein. He does not use dialogue with these philosophers for superficial confirmation of his own convictions. Aicher does not exploit his interlocutors. But he does not want merely to interpret them. Each of his dialogues opens up a new view of the philosopher addressed.

Aicher is not bound by historical exposition in his interpretation of philosophers like Ockham, Buridan, Descartes, Kant and Wittgenstein. But he does not disregard hermeneutic obligations. He is not concerned to imply that Ockham, Kant or Wittgenstein had intentions identical with his own. He simply takes up thoughts that convince him, independently of their historical context. This is particularly legitimate when we learn to understand something better, or for the first time.

Aicher and Wittgenstein share a common interest in architecture. Aicher sees the house that Wittgenstein built for his sister Gretl as a "school of making". He says that Wittgenstein, who built the house on the basis of the digital, logical severity of the *tractatus*, detected the flaws in this early philosophy as a result. Aicher sees the philosphy of use, of language games and life forms as being derived from Wittgenstein's experience as an architect.

There is no better example as this for Aicher's conviction that knowledge is the "reverse of making" and that making is "work on oneself". In Aicher's eyes Wittgenstein learned from his work as an architect that analogous thinking is superior to digital thinking.

Aicher's philosophical reflections are an introduction to design, creativity and developing. For him there is nothing that should not be designed, created and developed. This is true of one's own self, of life with others and with nature, the objects of everyday life, living and thinking. We acquire the ability to design and create by doing it. What we do and in what profession is secondary. We should simply not allow ourselves to be guided by pre-formed designs and previously devised plans.

Of course freedom to move free from prescriptions requires independence of judgement. Aicher sees his "visual thinking" as an element of the power of judgement, as Kant did imagination. We acquire the ability to judge correctly by learning to see and perceive correctly. This is not just true of designers, it is true of all of us.

In this context Aicher turns critically to designers and architects, and recommends that what they design should not be directed simply at function, but at materials and their organization. Form should do justice first of all to material and then to function. If this imperative is disregarded, then design degenerates into sales promotion and architecture becomes ornamental. Creation and design lose their autonomy and are determined and abused by economic and political purposes. Aicher does not see this kind of "aesthetic consumption" as an isolated phenomenon. It is an expression of the crisis in our self-perception that has parallel phenomena in all spheres of life.

Design, architecture and philosophy hardly relate to each other at all as academic disciplines. This is appropriate to their different tasks. But as Aicher shows, they have in common the problem of how thinking and making relate to each other. This is the problem of all kinds of design and creation. Aicher does not leave it at that insight. He recognizes that designing and creation have to satisfy a fundamental demand, that of human self-determination.

Critique of rationalism

Aicher's thinking is not limited to a philosophy of making. He does not only confront philosophical problems of cognition, sensual perception, language and thinking from a different point of view. If he prefers the analogous and concrete to the digital and abstract he does it with a philosophical intention. He relativizes the role of pure reason. He criticizes the rationality of Modernism as a result of the dominance of purely abstract thinking.

This critique has a political slant. Aicher sees the cultural and political consequences of the absolute claim of abstract reason. They have an effect on the institutions of our culture and the state. In his view the dominance of abstract thinking has been copied in the cultural and political circumstances of our age.

In criticizing rationalism, Aicher intends to criticize the claims of the institutions which consider themselves to be the agents of absolute values and truths. He considers the very claim that there are such values and truths to be absurd. Like Ockham's critique of universals, Aicher's critique of abstract thought is politically coherent.

Anyone who prefers the abstract to the concrete does not only misunderstand the mutual dependence of concept and view. In Aicher's judgement he is also creating a false hierarchy, a rank order that is culturally fatal. Things that are digital and abstract are not greater, higher and more important than things that are analogous and concrete.

Aicher is opposed to false hierarchies. His thinking is republican. He is concerned about the correct relationship between analogous and digital, the correct distribution of weight, priority in the right place, and in the right context. What is ordinary is not ordinary for him in a derogatory sense.

But the ordinary is also not extraordinary. It is the thing that is appropriate to the purposes of our daily lives. Ordinary things are determined by our use of things and not by aesthetic ideals. Design should take account of the ordinary, of the purposes of our lives. Design should serve practice, human life forms, and not dominate the use of things aesthetically.

For Aicher aestheticization of life appears particularly clearly in design that is directed not at use but at fine art. He compares this disregard of use and concrete practice with disregard of what is particular and empirical in certain traditions of metaphysics. If design takes fine art as a model it puts itself in the service of "aesthetic metaphysics". Aicher uses this name like a curse, similarly to the way in which Wittgenstein and the Vienna circle spoke about "metaphysics" and its apparent problems.

For Aicher the beautiful appearance of artistic design is not just an irritation. Design of this kind ignores human purposes and use, and thus also the demands of human life. It is a bürden on our lives in the same way that the rubbish we create is a burden on nature. Artistic design frivolously gives away the opportunity to shape the living world humanely.

Aicher's imperative is that we should redesign the world. In his thinking the world as design is the theme that connects design and philosophy directly. Design requires concrete developments, not abstract planning. We should not just be designing material objects such as houses and cities for living and working in, but developing and changing ourselves.

The changes in thinking and making demanded by Aicher have philosophical precedents. These are to be found above all in Ockham, Kant and Wittgenstein. Some of their basic insights have become central themes for Aicher. Ockham anchored true perception in the sensually concrete particular and not in the general. Kant identified the significance of imagination for our understanding of natural things. And finally Wittgenstein saw the meaning of what we say in the use of words and sentences. All three philosophers in their particular ways redesigned the world and altered thinking. Aicher repeatedly takes up their basic insights, varies them and combines them with his own reflections on the reason of the concrete when doing things.

Aicher today

Otl Aicher died after an accident in the late summer of 1991, much too soon, as they say. In the same year, two volumes containing many of his essays were published (*analog und digital, die welt als entwurf*). Another volume containing essays about current political topics was published posthumously (*schreiben und widersprechen*, Berlin 1993). If you take the three volumes that have been mentioned together with the books that he wrote and designed (e.g. with regard to typography, the subject of "light" and the many exhibitions and exhibition catalogues), the large bandwidth and tremendous variety of Aichers work becomes evident, ultimately that which he meant by "designing"" and "doing". He was also a designer in his work as an author, photographer and philosopher. Much of his work is well documented and easy to understand in a readworthy biography (Eva Moser: *Otl Aicher: Gestalter. Eine Biografie,* Ostfildern 2011).

Aicher's actions and thoughts have left traces behind which are evident in the work of many designers and architects in many countries, not just in Germany. The history of his influence cannot be portrayed in individual examples here, but one example of his influence that I remember was his collaboration with Norman Foster, which is documented in three large volumes and exemplary to a certain degree. The special nature of the work and design of the three volumes is described in a separate small volume (*Otl Aicher an der Arbeit für Norman Foster*, Ernst und Sohn 1989). On the one hand, the three volumes are a monograph of Fosters architecture (Vol. 1: 1964–1973,

Vol.2: 1971-1978, Vol.3: 1978-1985) which was originally intended to encompass five volumes, but remained incomplete due to Aicher's early demise. On the other hand, these volumes are a perfect example of how Aicher designed books, and the manifestation of that which the books were intended to show. They show what they say in the best way possible. Of course, this is expected from any well-designed book. In the case of architecture it is about something that appears easy to show, because architecture has to be seen, depends on pictures and can be brought to life with illustrations. Many illustrated books about architecture visualise that which appears to be easy to show but in a superficial way, as though they were advertising brochures. They show pictures of building projects and buildings and also name them, but otherwise they say very little. They do not end up in the awkward situation of also showing what they are saying. The three volumes about Fosters architecture are quite different. The projects and buildings are described in detail by many authors, many of whom who collaborated on the projects. We are not talking about superficiality, instead the genealogies and structures of Foster's architecture are shown, described and explained. You can see and read how drawings are turned into structures, how they blend into landscapes and ensembles and turn them into something remarkable.

Aicher explained his approach of the three volumes as follows: "It was not the structures that I saw first, but the way in which they were created. Here you could see what architecture is in which thinking is not just allowed (. . .), but is created by thinking . . . " (*Otl Aicher on the work for Norman Foster,* 8). Aichers critical but also architectural spirit is between the lines. In the monograph about Foster's architecture he objects to portrayals in which the architecture comes along "as though it came off a catwalk" (loc. cit.). He criticises architecture that follows fashions and ideas. Instead he demands buildings that are justified and can be justified, like those of Foster.

There is another reason for remembering the design of the Foster monograph. It shows how Aicher designed books. He defines an exact line break matrix, an organisation principle of design. The typography and layout are precisely organised. All of this together makes that which Aicher called the syntax of design. Like the use of a language, the syntax must not be in the spotlight, and must not stand out. And it does not stand out. It is merely noticeable how clear and understandable the process descriptions of the construction projects are, and how clear the connections between the pictures and the texts are. The principles of design upon which the three-volume monograph are based are unsurpassed in the design that was used by Aicher.

Wilhelm Vossenkuhl
Munich 1991/2014

grasping with the hand and mind

the relationship between thinking and body is so close that what happens in the mind is often described in the language of the hands. mind is often seated less in transcendence than in the hand. because the hand can grasp, thought can also grasp. because our hand can take hold of something our heads can take hold of it as well. because the hand can present, thinking can represent. because the hand can lay things down, thinking can lay things down as well. and we do not just lay things down, we overlay, lay things on top of each other. we do not just set things firmly in mind, we set things up, a new theory for example. we do not just grasp, do not just take hold, we take a view of things, twist them and turn them and finally arrive at a point of view.

having grasped something mentally is not just a pictorial analogy with physical grasping. the culture of thinking requires a culture of the hand as a subtle, sensitive organ. if the hand can open up, if it doesn't just work, but plays as well, if it perceives, than the mind will open up more freely as well. the hand's plasticity is the plasticity of thought. the concept is what is conceived.

only with the eye, with seeing, do we associate a similar abundance of words and concepts to describe thought processes. we look through and survey, we develop views of the world, perspectives and points of view.

our natural languages can be evaluated archaeologically, under their words lie the ruins of earlier relationships, earlier developments. words conceal their own ruins.

if one understands language in this way as evidence for the way in which the evolution of thought might have developed, then mind will be seen only as a station on the closed loop that makes thinking, along with the hand and the eye the station of control and comparison, in other words evaluation. understanding, eye and hand are to be seen in a linked circle of effectiveness.

thinking emerged from the control function in the closed loop of making. anyone threading a needle with his hand takes the thread to the eye of the needle with his fingers. if you miss, the eye signals the result to the brain, this passes a control order to the hand

and the closed loop can start again. action, control and conclusion are a linked process so characteristic of everything that lives that it can be considered defined by that process.

modern thinking has started to concern itself with the laws of thinking, of counting, of systematization and drawing conclusions in a new way, one that is detached from the real world, abstract. this led to the fact that we have as good as disconnected seeing and acting as prerequisites of thinking. the algebrization of the world made us take formulae, thought processes and logical operations for granted and established them as a way of thinking about thinking. the mind woke up as a mind. we can even understand mathematical laws if we understand nothing else. the closed loop has largely been reduced to the inner world of reason.

but is the inner world of reason the whole world? today, when we are stuck in the thousand culs-de-sac of this immanent reason, we are rediscovering the eye, rediscovering the hand. we are rediscovering the domain of making as a prerequisite of thought.

we are discovering that thinking was liberated because the human hand was liberated. when human beings, at a certain stage of their development, came out of the forests, their hands became superfluous as catching organs. they were free, and man learned to use them for other tasks, certainly playfully at first, then with control, pragmatically adapted to his new situation.

physiologically this change was clearly expressed in the development of the opposable thumb. before it became opposable the thumb was set parallel to the other fingers, and the hand was only useful for swinging from branch to branch: when moving hand over hand, the hand has to be shaped like a hinge. when the thumb is set opposite the other four fingers the hand can take hold of things, can grip: pick up sticks and stones and do things with them. the passive catching hand becomes an active gripping hand, an unspecific, variable instrument.

and it becomes a playing hand. we can still imagine what happened when man at a certain stage of his development picked something up and twisted and turned it, with a hand that was not an animal extremity, but free to grasp and clutch; we can imagine how something like an evaluatory insight came about here. and now it was not just the situation that determined man's actions, he was not only in direct contact with his environment via instincts, but able to control himself through his own insights.

control of the thumb in its new role required an enormous increase in brain growth. the functions the thumb has to perform are so varied that the organizing mass of the brain was enlarged. life outside the forests at the same time demanded growth in communication. people lived on the surface in small family groups. unlike antelopes they did not have the possibility of running away, they had to defend their existence on the spot, also regulate their continuing life in the small group and needed to co-operate more to be able to do this.

both development of the hand and development of language needed an organizational repertoire in the brain.

a new methodological principle was necessary to do justice to the new situation.

the human brain consists of two halves, perhaps as a result of the duality of arms, legs, ears, eyes. Each half of the brain controls half of each pair of organs. like man the brain is double. and the two halves control the two halves of the body like brothers. the brothers are such close colleagues that one can take over the other's tasks.

in the course of their development there was a time when the demands made on the brothers were too heavy. they could not manage the role of the hand and the new communication role in harmony. appeals to nature for, shall we say, expansion of the firm were ignored. there were no more core memory stores.

and so the only possible option was division of labour. the brothers decided that each would not independently do parallel jobs, but new ones of their own.

this too is an entirely viable principle of evolution: instead of two halves doing the same thing analogously, each half takes on a new task. one is the business manager and the other the economist.

this step was of course only possible because a reserve existed. the dual parallelism of the central nervous system, the doubling in the interest of the validation of one part against the other contained a niche of evolution.

was nature making a mistake here? there are theories that say there was no other choice. even the growth of the brain to this point had a significant consequence. people with heads that are too large cannot be born, the structure of the body does not permit it. the consequence is that man comes into the world as a kind of premature birth, with a skull that is not fully developed.

almost all animals can move in every way as soon as they come into the world. ducks swim, birds fly, young horses stand on their legs after a day. man would have to stay in the womb for twenty months to reach this stage of development, but would then not be capable of being born.

and so as the skull could not be programmed to grow, meaning that expansion of each half of the brain was not possible, only the principle of differentiation remained. since then man has been a living creature with an inner split. but this was in the interest of optimizing his performance.

from the point at which this condition obtained, we are dealing with man. this is where the difference from pre-nature lies. it quickly had practical consequences. the new man who had come out of the forests could use only one hand and one arm fully. fighting with wild animals, and also preparation of food was generally possible with the right arm only.

this left the other half of the brain free to build up a language centre and acquire calculating thought. loss of the usable left hand was compensated for by a transfer of work to language and analytical thought.

the loss this caused is not tragic. nature also permitted a number of lefthanded people, so that social organization of left and right is guaranteed. the degree of success is enormous, work sharing is stimulating, not only in recent times. two separate parts of the brain that can replace each other but take up tasks of their own are a new evolutionary programme.

the functions of the brain, the volume of the thinkable have increased. what is the disadvantage of being able to use only one hand or one foot with the virtuosity needed by a fully developed body? we have been somewhat limited in our way of moving since then. something over 90% of people are right-handed and can play ball games only with their right hand. 9% are left-handed, and a very few have retained early man's ability to use both hands and both feet with equal virtuosity. additionally the human hand is much more developed than that of man's forbears. they would never have been able to sew, write or play an instrument. perhaps this acquisition of dexterity also meant that only one hand is in a position to hammer in a nail or direct a paintbrush. in any case reduction of the control function of the brain has created additional scope.

as i have said, the disadvantage is that our consciousness has been split since then. man is a split being, a being of inward as well as outward conflict. this conflict became greater when the different halves of man were further differentiated, and this differentiation began to have an effect on social organization. we are thinkers, we are craftsmen, we are pragmatists and we are analysts. we are scientists and technicians. we are semanticists and syntacticists. we are abstract and concrete . . .

another division into two, if not a split, had already taken place in the division that we now indiscriminately call the division between body and mind. originally each cell controlled itself. later there was a division between control cells and performing cells, the motor cells. certainly body and mind are a whole and interdependent, but the differentiation that came about also produced conflict and a compulsion towards a life skill of compensation. the life story of a particular human being is full of echoes of conflicts caused by differentiation of this kind. everybody's psyche is full of scars. no life passes without neurotic disturbances, often the painful conflicts of a divided human being.

the split in our brain into two hemispheres does not yet seem problematical to us today. so far we have managed to live with it, also with the reduction of full bodily powers to just one side, which essentially is the same as a slight paralysis of our hands and feet. but the conflict can become important, as can the division of man and woman, body and mind.

what will become of a computer civilization of calculating and counting operating only digitally, replacing qualities of the living with qualities that can be counted? replacing the living with total technology, and experience with accountability? so overworking logical calculation and the formalism of conclusion-drawing that no direct insights are possible any more, like insights of use and making, insights of eye and hand? are we not on the threshold of an age that places calculation before appreciation?

it will probably carry little conviction to suggest a false development of evolution immediately it has settled for a single principle. digitalization of the world is in full swing. it has taken things as far as technical manipulation of hereditary characteristics, thus as far as synthetic beings.

on the other hand, the range of human experience is getting bigger today as well. there is a hunger for perceptions derived from experience of one's own doing, from personal intervention. people are abandoning general programmes to realize themselves. they are giving up abstract idealism and looking for determination within themselves. the more precisely and perfectly industry works, the more people are looking for work that they produce themselves, independently of perfection.

it is precisely those people who see rationality as a virtue who employ it again in the physical field of relationship of seeing and making. it is precisely those who are concerned about the mind who are concerned about physicality. there are signs that people want to grasp the world again. the mind is not longer rooted in transcendence. thinking is no longer so much formalized logic, not digitalized calculating, but the attempt to grasp something. grasping something, is that not the language of the hand again? do we not really grasp only that which we can hold?

philosophy discovers use as the source of perception, logic has got itself tangled up in paradoxes. it stands in front of black walls and either looks for ladders to climb over them or thinks of cognition by that which can be experienced, can be made, can be used.

extensions of the ego

in our linguistic usage there are only three categories for human stature, there is physical stature, personal stature in terms of character, and stature in terms of social and historical importance.
napoleon was small, only 1.63 m tall. if his woman of the bedchamber madame de rebusat is to be believed, he must have had a terrible character, but he remains a fixed star in the historical firmament.
a fully grown person today is between 1.50 and 2 metres tall. if one could find out the height of all adults, it would be possible to work out an average height. perhaps 1.738320 m, but that would be uninteresting. each person is only his own height. the statistical average is only an arithmetical height that can occasionally say something, for example whether people are getting larger or smaller, to the extent that the appropriate comparative figures are available. otherwise each person is autonomous and unique in his height, but we do not perceive it precisely, just in classifications like large, medium, small. for the course of a person's life precise height is not significant. it is only entered in passports in the interests of the state's ability to identify.
stature in terms of character and morality is perhaps less vague than people think. one is pretty well aware who is a scoundrel, an opportunist, a good mate or a good, faithful soul. one knows who is a good chap. these standards are used independently of education, professional standing and zeitgeist, right down to little lads' street friendships. we know fairly quickly how we stand as this experience is common to everyone, professors, bankers, charwomen and ladies of the street. the chosen official moral code plays a subordinate role, social behaviour is open to immediate experience and is registered qualitatively.
historical stature is extremely relative. in the age of saints the saint is great, in the age of the warrior the physical hero is great, in the age of the nationalist state the general is prince and leader, and at a time of enlightenment the writer and philosopher takes charge. all the great men of history are the product of interest situations. how much longer will napoleon and bismarck remain fixed stars in the firmament of history? when their light wanes we should not disregard the fact that there are other great men who have

already been forgotten, even some who were worshipped as gods.

here there is a gap in our linguistic usage. there is another dimension of human stature that we do not express directly in language.

the stature that does not appear in our linguistic usage, that still does not have a place in our consciousness, could be the actual stature of human beings.

a violinist extends his two arms and hands by adding a device, a violin and its bow. this produces music, something human. how long is his arm? is the instrument part of it? is it a part, an extension of his body, or is it an alien object like a parcel delivered by the post office?

a painter who is painting can only paint with a paintbrush; and a writer who is writing needs something to write with, a fountain pen, a typewriter or a word processor.

for a secretary a typewriter could be a random object that she may not even like. for a writer it is part of him. perhaps a kind of artificial limb, a kind of additional organ. his body does not end at his fingers. his fingers are only effective by means of a technical extension.

perhaps his hands are quiet and indifferent all day. they are involved in washing, dressing, eating, but they only come alive when they are typing thoughts. then the physical bounds of a human being are not determined by his body but by his devices.

what is a shoemaker's hand without hammer and knife, what an electrical fitter's hand without screwdriver and pliers?

an animal lives in time but has no awareness of time. we live in time with the assistance of the watch on our wrist. by dividing up time we make it open to experience. if there were no measuring rods there would be no lengths.

we are experiencing the bounds and limitations of human senses and organs in terms of radioactivity in a fatal way. we cannot perceive it, and are overwhelmed with fear and anxiety all over the world when a nuclear reactor cracks. we have to extend our ability to perceive by the use of indicating devices. perhaps we'll soon have a geiger counter next to the barometer in our homes, or wear a miniature one on our wrist like a watch, because we have become suspicious of the people who govern us. we are not complete and installed in our humanity without devices for making or communicating. human beings, every single one, develop by the standards of their individual devices, their tools, their indicators, if not their machines and apparatus.

as soon as the potter's wheel became available the individual was extended and learned to organize supplies using pots and containers. using hand tools, axes, saws and hammers, man withdrew from nature into homes. he built cities and cathedrals. it was not really until today, when car and bicycle have made him more mobile, that he has started to do justice to his essence through his artefacts, his artificial limbs and the extension of his organs to an extent as well. the craft age extended his creativity. today he has not only developed greater external mobility, but also greater internal mobility.

if self-determination is the essence of man, rather than being bound up with nature, then humanity is only possible with the aid of devices of all kinds. it is not a constraint but an extension of our own possibilities if every human being learns to handle pen and paper, acquires reading and writing skills.

it is not a constraint, but a great self-realization if we prepare food on the stove in boiling saucepans and hot frying pans and eat it in a different, artificial condition.

could we go back to the idea of eating with our fingers again, doing without knife, fork and spoon? if we did, we could live only on what we could pick up in our hands. the art of cooking would be lost, and with it something that makes men different from animals.

cooking has its roots in food conservation, in the storage of provisions. but it has become something more, a field in which humanity is established. humanity means being creative of one's own accord, setting one's own aims. every meal that we prepare is an attempt to do something as well as possible, either a dish that tastes as good as grandmother's, or even a new one. some food is a declaration of love.

and if there were no scissors? how would we make our clothes? would we wear clothes at all? our ability to adapt to climate would be reduced, and we would lose our pleasure in fabrics, colours and patterns. and we do not need only needle and scissors, we need loom and spinning wheel, although today in a kind of co-operative organization-form.

a spider is not just a spider in terms of its body, its web is part of it as well. it would starve without a web. so what is a spider? is it a living creature or is it a living creature plus catching device? is it singular, or the centre of a system that is only capable of survival as a whole? we can only see the spider in association with the web that it produces, as a life system, not a living creature. the spider is an organizational form. it is only itself with the assistance of a kind of extended, web-like arm. web and spider belong together.

man too is not an isolated body. he is not contained in his biological physicality. he is the total of his device, his work, his culture, his organization-form. he does not exist, he sets himself up. work is his purpose. and this not as a fate, but as a prerequisite of himself, as a realization of himself.

st. thomas aquinas recognized that the grace of god requires the nature of man. st. thomas aquinas would have to formulate that differently today. he would have to say that grace requires culture.

man is not just a natural being. st. thomas aquinas follows aristotle. for aristotle experience is the prerequisite of perception; for us the prerequisite of perception is our own making. perception is comparison. of course this is also true for us today; but we have active perception, as we compare through doing.

man has the perceptions of a cultural being, not a natural being. the loop that consists of making, comparing and correcting, in order to lead into another one that again consists of (corrected) making, comparing and correcting, makes creative and cultural thinking possible. this thinking is not only receptive, but projective. it consists of drafts and schemes, thrusts into the unknown.

self-confident thinking in making leads in self-organized steps to new data outside natural contexts. they have to be expressed in language. making something, fixing it in language and talking about it, that is culture.

at first this making, thinking and speaking serve the balance of our immediate environment. we build houses to protect ourselves from rain and cold. we preserve food for seasons in which there is nothing to harvest. and we make clothes that resist rain and frost. and we do all this not as an instinctive reaction, but as a self-determined action.

but we do more as well. we do not want to make only what is necessary, but what can be made, we do not want to think merely of ecological, of practically compelling things, we want to think what is thinkable, we want to say not only things that serve as information, but things that can be said. we discover that we are less bound into a pre-existing reality than facing the openness of free spaces. we do not just design ourselves into the temporal future, but also transcend the bounds of the given world to reach new possibilities. piece by piece we build the structure that translates the possible into new reality, into made reality.

man is in a process of becoming. he is a state, a case, a situation. we recognize his open bounds. man has no final being. he is a current organization-form, a current life-state.

states are manufactured, made. we reach new states by manufacturing devices and organization-forms. by making we develop from being an autonomous subject to a being that plays, invents, develops, and thus acquires the tools that make the world of rigid being into a world of conditions. man is his life-form.

awareness of this paradoxically increases with the dangers that arise from this insight.

the world is increasingly endangered with autonomy of making and of thinking. the made world is not good in itself. making leads into the unknown and is as wrong as it is right.

as we become aware of the endangered life situation we also become aware that we exist in situations, that we are a condition, not beings, not existences. but every situation is critical.

in just one generation we have had to acknowledge how wonderful and how dreadful the motor car is. appraisal of our artefacts is taking great steps forward. and awareness of confusion about what we have done is growing to the same extent.

it does not mean a lot today to make a beautiful product, a beautiful building, a beautiful picture, a beautiful book. there are no more individual objects when we have to acknowledge that we live in particular conditions and circumstances. the work of art on the wall stops being helpful when we have to seek a life-form that is tolerable as a whole. life itself has become art.

there is no longer a lot of point in distinguishing between subject and object. we are in our objects and our objects are us. it used to be possible to surround oneself with objects, one could collect art. today we have ourselves become the subject of art, the entanglement of subject and objects. we know that we can no longer separate our ego and our immediate surroundings. we can no longer furnish ourselves at random, as collectors used to furnish themselves with art, we are ourselves the furnished things.

we have fallen into a made world that we did not want to make like that. we have to become aware of making. we have to make ourselves aware and do that awarely. our mistakes are the prerequisites of our changes.

we have to learn to understand that we are beings that live from our artefacts, and from what we do with them. we are part of the artefacts to the extent that they are part of us. the mind is not in the intellect, but in physicality, in its realization as acting and making. the mind is not in the general, but in what is concrete and made.

thinking serves insight, serves perception. thinking about thinking reaches another dimension, makes meaning accessible. it establishes what is meaningful.

but in a made world an aim is only binding in draft and in experiment, the concretization of a general value. values and value systems are general. but the general is only binding to the extent that it becomes a reality of life. the general is something like a realization. it is dangerous to believe in freedom as individuals are advised to do today. law and freedom are, so it is said, sufficiently noble values in themselves. However, freedom and law are only concrete freedom and concrete law. and as a made world leads to constantly new conditions of furnishing, the temptation to standardization and arrangement in controllable systems is constantly growing. freedom and with it law do not exist, on the contrary, they are in constant danger and can therefore only be found in concrete freedom and concrete law, in the assertion that can be lived, in designed realization. in truth the idealization of freedom and law is merely a distraction from its existence-form, it takes place only as a distraction and to make manipulation from above easier. only a society that is directed and connected by generalized thought can be controlled from above. we know today that humanity cannot be planned. no-one talks of command economies any more. but people believe all the more that it would be possible to make such a system work, which comes down to the same thing.

if man is understood as a self-determining, self-controlling being, the limiting point must be made that in many respects we are directly bound up in prescribed natural events. we have no direct influence on how our bodies process their food. self-preservation and reproduction are external life-control systems. they affect the self-determining ego, but do not originate from it.

it is equally true that there is feedback from the conscious ego to our motor life-factors as well. the body takes in prepared food, almost exclusively. its vegetative, even more its psychological domain, is not autonomous. when there are difficulties of agreement, whether between intellect and psyche and psyche and purely biological motor systems, or between conscious ego and physicality, then the complication we call illness occurs.

as a result of his self-control, man is a being who knows illness, unlike animals. they are fundamentally healthy. man is fundamentally sick. his ability to realize himself does not have frictionless transmission. automatism has been lost.

as individuals we are always close to illness and as a society we are plagued by illness. our commerce and technology are fundamentally sick because doing things oneself and self-determination lie outside nature. we have eaten of the tree of the knowledge of good and evil. and thus we are determined by our work, realization in doing. and work is not nature, even if it is in ecological harmony with nature.

making is not activism. all right, there are perversions of making, bustle, just as there are perversions of thinking, withdrawals into ideality. the dangers of activism must not be ignored. commercialism is making for the sake of making, a frantic bustle deprived of the dimension of meaning, amputated, for the optimization of commercial success.

and this too is correct: space for personal activity is getting smaller and smaller. what does there remain for me to do when my house, my food, my clothes are delivered as ready-made products, and so are news, contracts and party-political programmes? who is so privileged as to be able to set up his own life?

a family once agreed that they would give each other only things that they had made themselves for birthdays and christmas. they didn't like seeing impersonal goods piled up under the christmas tree, the extravagance of which increased with the insipid feeling of not having made any personal contribution.

the effect was unusual, the criterion of the presents was no longer size, number and quantity. they were forced to remain modest, but more aware, intensive and personal.

the important thing was not so much that more pleasure was given. the giver was himself the recipient. he painted, drew, wrote, created poetry, made little books, invented new games, suddenly collected things that he wouldn't have glanced at before.

continued over the years this changed the personality of the maker himself. the little book became a bigger book, then a big book. in the end an author emerged who would never have written a book that could have been sold on the book market while working at the same time. and children developed a knowledge of their talents that allowed them to take up a profession of their own, instead of having it prescribed by the state of the economy.

it does not matter what one does to develop one's own self. it is clear that not everyone can do everything, and probably shouldn't. it is only when one's own development is under way that one begins to be self-contained, to develop one's own mind, where others need psychosomatic assistance on the basis of the fact that environment and ego cannot be united.

the prerequisite is that one does not do something for the sake of an achievement, does not make something to put it on to the market, to show off in front of other people and to get rich from it. making is itself the meaning of making, just as it is the privilege of the scientist to do research for research's sake. method itself is revelation. output is the result of input. what comes out of it simply arises, it is not looked for.

the eye, visual thinking

i was there when the word *kommunikation* was introduced into the german language. we have only been using it for about thirty years. in the mean time it has become a key word for the understanding of this century.

it was in a staff room in the hochschule für gestaltung in ulm, and we were looking for a term to cover advertising, propaganda, language, persuasion and publicity. we fell back on the english concepts of visual and verbal communication and used them to label the appropriate departments and spheres of work.

shortly after this the culture and education committee of the regional parliament of baden-württemberg came to ulm to investigate whether this college, which in the mean time has become legendary, was worthy of support. the representatives of culture and education asked what *kommunikation* was. whether it had anything to do with communism or even communion.

the hochschule für gestaltung was closed at the behest of the politicians, the politicians are still in office, the word did its rounds. it has become a favourite word among politicians. that's how times are.

the phenomenon of communication is new. the word has made us aware of a particular state of affairs in modern society. posters have existed only since the time of toulouse-lautrec. since then we have photography and film, illustrated papers, reportage. it is above all in visual language that we discover the phenomenon of communication and also verbal communication, language, has been seen more markedly since then from the point of view of its social transmission of ideas, from person to person. previously the criterion of its quality was more likely to be poetry, the poetic word, and less comprehensibility and the breadth of what is conveyed. it was assessed aesthetically, not as social dialogue.

discovery of the picture has made us aware that we have entered an age of communication. society becomes a phenomenon of communication, can only be properly understood through communication. the social element of society is its constant exchange of information, the production of constantly new awareness content.

and while marx still saw exploitation above all from the point of view of material production, the economy, michel foucault reflects about the fact that power could above all be the power of information. power is administration of knowledge and the creation of powerful knowledge.

the 18th and 19th centuries were an epoch of language, of theory, of history of thinking in terms of cause and effect. it is the epoch of classicism, of exact sciences and the first phase of the technical revolution, of mechanics, of the conversion of energy. it is an epoch starved of pictures. perhaps a reaction to the age of absolutism and of the baroque, as subjects' heads were filled with a flood of pictures, of church and palace façades.

the renaissance thinks in pictures, in views and insights, in perspectives. but at the beginning of the modern age stands a man who denigrated seeing and introduced a period that manages without seeing, rené descartes. art falls back from the formulation of points of view and opinions confirming classical antiquity as the ideal of a rational, descriptive culture. poets and thinkers, philosophers, mathematicians and scientists determine the claims of culture. communication is reduced to an extreme extent. what counted was not dialogue, the exchange of ideas, but proofs, conclusions, proclamation, freedom from contradiction for theory. we only became aware of what communication is again through the discovery of the picture. another, new power to convince joined the logical conclusion, and that was evidence. pictures are not necessary for thought, but absolute. they do not have to convince, they are authentic. we have come to rely upon the picture again for our assessment of the world.

animals have languages. but they do not have pictures. they can express themselves in signs, in signals, but producing pictures is alien to them. only man can double the world by creating a picture.

medical investigation of the eye also runs parallel to the discovery of the picture. helmholtz, a contemporary of toulouse-lautrec, invented the ophthalmoscope, which makes it possible to examine the back of the eye. he developed the scientific theory of sight.

even rené descartes had made experimental studies of the eye using the eyes of cattle, which he cut open. one of the demands of science at his time was that mathematicians and philosophers should also be concerned with physics and medicine.

descartes was interested in the eye as an organ of perception. he studied the way in which it functioned as a kind of biological camera. he was also interested in the notion that our senses deceive us, and that only pure thought can be relied upon, something separate from the phenomenon as we receive it from a sensory organ. i think therefore i am. body is material, limited, imperfect. this is how descartes justified the rationalism upon which modern science and modern technology are based.

this rationalism is increasingly falling into disrepute, and with it the reduction of all processes to cause and effect and their interpretation from elemental laws. galilei started to ban concepts like force, substance and influence from the analysis of natural phenomena and to admit only dimensions that could be objectivized like weight, time and distance. descartes even reduced geometry to numerical values by developing curves from formulae. the formula for the parabola is $y2 = 2px$. the curve, the phenomenon, had disappeared, but the numerical equation remained. a world, a technology and a mechanics that could be calculated had opened up.

natural events dissolved into natural laws, products into financial values, life risk to an insurance value. art is even quoted on the stock exchange today.

man a machine, the eye a camera. contemporaries of descartes were newton, who discovered the mechanics of the heavens, huygens, who developed the wave theory of light. the discovery of the telescope and microscope in those days put scientists on the track of laws of optics and the techniques of lens arrangement. everything indicated that the eye is a camera.

i am making a great leap to our own times and to a modern city. until quite recently the eye surgeon meyer-schwickerat, recognized internationally because of his technique of operating on the retina with a beam of sharply focused light, was working in essen. a number of years ago i read a remark of his that seemed, perhaps less to him than to me, to be a reversal of values. he said that when he was operating on the eye he was operating on the brain. the eye is part of the brain.

i was electrified by this remark, because on the basis of my work as a graphic designer i had at an early stage come to the conviction that we use not only logical and calculating thought, but thought that takes place in pictures, visual thought. in the fifties this was still in stark contrast with the scientific traditions of the modern age. according to this, perception and thinking are two different things. sensual perception belongs to the body, thought is an activity of the mind.

in the nineteen-fifties the american scientist adalbert ames once more tried to prove something that descartes had already formulated, that our senses deceive us. to this end he created a series of famous experimental models, some of which produced amazing results.

you looked through a peephole into a room in which two friends were each standing in a corner, one of them small as a dwarf, the other, smiling and twinkly-eyed, as large as a giant. you put a hand to your head. these were friends that you had just been talking to, and now one was half the size of the other.

but the explanation was quite simple as soon as you looked at the way the experiment was arranged from the side. the space you were looking into was distorted. one corner of the room was near the peephole and low, the other a long way away and high. in one position a man scarcely had room to stand, in the other he looked lost. both corners, the near one and the far one, were so arranged in terms of height that they seemed the same from the peephole.

this very quickly turned me against adalbert ames. if he had arranged the experiment in such a way that you could look through two holes with two eyes, with the help of parallax, the difference in depth of focus, you would have seen immediately that the room was distorted. or if he had permitted the eye to observe not just from one point only, but with a slight movement to and fro, then again you would have seen the distortion immediately. but as it was the proof worked only when looking with one eye through a fixed hole with a fixed viewpoint. Is this really how people see?

the inference from this experiment was disillusioning. man sees three-dimensionally with two eyes, and he sees with constant variation in viewpoint. man simply does not see like a camera. for seeing you need two cameras in constant motion. the experiment dug its own grave of scientific reduction and fell into it.

seeing is much more complicated than the arrangement of a series of optical-physical experiments makes it seem.

the eye is an organ of a living being, and we have a form of seeing appropriate to a living being. in fact it

american sociologist adalbert ames wanted to prove, like descartes, that our senses deceive us. he built rooms in which living human beings seemed to be different heights when viewed through a peephole looking into the room. in fact the people are simply in different distances from the viewer. ames achieved the appropriate spatial deception by distorted spatial structures. if the viewer can see through two peepholes, or if it is possible for his eye to move somewhat to the side, the trick is quickly revealed. that is how reliable our perceptions are.

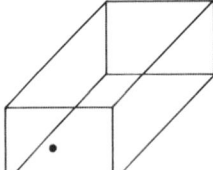 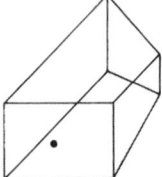

is not a matter of an organ, the eye, but of a process, seeing.

if things are taken like this, then meyer-schwickerat's assertion is confirmed. he is not operating on the eye, but on a part of the brain. in fact we do not see with the eye but with the brain. optical signals are all that is admitted by the eye, physical data, like light and dark, colours from red to violet.

with the eye we see trees, a large number of trees. with the brain we see a wood. there was no such colour as turquoise until the 18th century. it did not become something that could be perceived until it was named, defined intellectually. this indicates that seeing is not just an achievement of the brain, but also a cultural achievement. we see things that culture has prepared as worth seeing.

according to this the eye is only the instrument that translates light waves into electronic neuron impulses. the different wave impulses admitted by the pupil are transmitted as nerve signals to the parts of the brain that manage seeing.

there are two aspects in the foreground. one is that we cannot possibly see everything that is admitted through pupil and lens and transmitted to the back of the eye. if a speaker is standing in a room the eye of course takes in all the optical data like space, light, other people, lectern, background, side walls. but in reality we see only the speaker. in other words our brain, our consciousness, is selective. it limits the view to what we want to see.

secondly, what we see is compared with stored data in our brain, which is at the same time the seat of our memory. we see against the background of our knowledge.

is the speaker credible? does he strike false notes? is he boring? everyone sees the speaker differently, according to the background of his experience and knowledge. and so we see by thinking and think by seeing. seeing is a specific form of thinking. i see, therefore i think.

and so does this mean that a blind man would not be able to think? in fact a blind man also has an inner view independent of the eye. if he feels a matchbox he experiences its shape and places it in a spatial world of top and bottom, front and back, left and right. for the blind man too, who does not perceive surfaces
that are seen with the eye, but probably spaces and situations, it is still valid to say: i see, therefore i think.

against the background of glorification of the mind and the things of the mind as opposed to the body this is a bold formulation. it would make thinking a form of physicality. we would no longer be able to divide the world into mind and matter.

we are fairly close to the eye of the typhoon, fairly near to the pivotal point from which a false past can be turned upside-down.

descartes said that reliable thinking should operate without the senses. we have realized that seeing and thinking are linked.

the eye is part of the brain. this remark by meyerschwickerat does not interest me merely as an insight, as a piece of scientific perception. it stimulates me to ask new questions, to set off along new paths.

since reading this sentence i have understood better why people look into each other's eyes when they meet. theoretically we could look at the ears or the nose. both are openings in the body like the eye. if we look at the mouth we are looking at the mouth. if we look into each other's eyes we are looking into the self, the person. if a mother wants to know the truth she tells her child to look her in the eye. the child speaks through its eyes, not through its mouth. two passers-by who do not know each other catch each other's eye in the street. if their eyes meet, it is an encounter. death sets in on the deathbed when the light in the eyes goes out. the eye may still be open, but it is not looking any more. i can look at a woman's hand. it remains an object, however beautiful it is. if i catch her eye, there she is the person that she is.

in seeing you perceive something that transcends abstract thought.

the modern age, the age of reason, begins with the extension of seeing. della porta invented the telescope in 1590, the dutch janssen brothers built the first microscope a few years later. the earliest scientific discipline was optics, the theory of refraction and diffraction of light using lens systems. kepler, descartes and newton created the theoretical framework. this also reduces human sight to a physical and optical process. the eye is understood as an optical instrument, like a camera.

today we adopt a quite different position. it is no longer the eye as an organ that is central, but seeing as a process, a complex system of perceiving, seeing, grasping, recognizing and thinking. we no longer stop at the material, mechanistic basis of seeing, the seeing instrument, but attempt to grasp seeing as a function. in the last resort it is not the eye that sees, but a system in which eye, brain, memory and learning, cultural training are involved.

the eye does not see, man sees. for example, the greeks did not have a word for the colour green. as a result of this the people of greek antiquity saw no green. of course the light waves that correspond to green entered their eyes, but they were not registered, they were not seen. this suggests that seeing takes place in the brain rather than the eye.

the mechanistic view of seeing, reduction of the eye to a camera, was overcome from two sides: once from the point of view of neurophysiology, especially brain research, and then from the point of view of behavioural research, in other words the question of how the eye reacts to its environment, its seeing reality, what mechanisms does it develop in order correctly to bring its object, the outside world, inside.

there are essays on the last point by erich von holst, a former colleague of konrad lorenz. he takes up observations made by helmholtz and produces a theory of seeing that is an experience for anyone who wants to know how we grasp what we call reality. is it reality, is it an illusion? i mention only that we see colours that do not exist in reality, purple for example.

purple is an aid to the correction apparatus that modifies pure sensory impressions in favour of correct apprehension of the outside world.

the actual physiological process of seeing is controlled, checked and actively influenced by the brain, the eye as a physical sensory organ alone would actually deceive us.

erich von holst describes a whole cosmos of seeing that takes place behind the retina, in the sight centre of the brain, thus correcting the purely physiological interpretation of seeing. a living creature will do anything to prevent being deceived by seeing. for example it always sees with two eyes rather than one (which was apparently not noticed until our century, otherwise demonstrations like ames' would never have been recognized as a serious scientific basis).

the extent to which the brain is involved in seeing has been revealed in an almost dramatic way from another point of view. much more attention has been paid to the consequences of brain injuries in the last three decades. brain medicine has reached some quite unusual insights in this way.

it is known that the process of seeing goes right through to the rear lobe of the brain, to the part that makes us see stars if we fall on the back of our head. this means that the process of seeing runs through the whole brain to its rear section. in this way the brain as a whole is activated.

and now brain medicine asserts that the brain is not only involved in seeing, but that the brain is an organ of picture manufacture and processing. it is stocked with pictures because it sees and judges in pictures, the brain compares pictures.

certainly this happens only in one half of the brain, in the right hemisphere. the brain does not only control seeing, it lives through seeing. it is there to see. the brain is also an organ of sight. the brain is an eye with a pictorial archive. accordingly thinking could be described as the comparison of pictures. some that you are seeing at the time, and others that you have seen before.

this state of affairs is all the more exciting as brain research has revealed that the other hemisphere, the left one, has a language centre that has an entirely different structure of perception. it does not see in pictures but reads in sentences. it thinks in a linear fashion, from word to word, from concept to concept, from conclusion to conclusion. it is an algebraic, not a geometrical brain.

of course most words are pictures, and a flow of pictures is engendered by hearing language. but it is grammar, arrangement of the words, connection, that creates meaning.

pictorial thinking is not linear, it sees surfaces, pictures, cards, diagrams. it does not draw conclusions, it sees links, relations, connections, analogies.

expressed in concepts of modern technology, we can say we have a digital brain and an analogous brain. in one of them lives descartes, in the other blaise pascal, who, himself a mathematician, physicist and engineer, even at that time led other insights into the field against reason, those of the heart, for example.

man has two different halves to his brain. originally they were just double, like our kidneys or our lungs. now they have specialized, as a result of the transition from natural being to cultural being. since then we also have two different hands. the right hand belongs to the left hemisphere of the brain, where language is localized, we write with our right hand. but we play the violin with our left hand, we finger the strings not according to causal chains, but according to proportions, connection fields, areas to be covered, by analogies.

all these are just suggestions. there is a great deal of detail to fill in. also that other creatures grasp their evidence with other sensory organs, not with the eye. it is not only light waves that form reality, but sound waves or heat radiation. a blind man cannot see, and so has to resort to other sensory data. but what emerges very clearly is that the crisis of rational thought turns out to be that it tried to eliminate seeing as an element of thought.

here we should remember the aged goethe, who conducted a life-long struggle against newton because he did not think that seeing, including the physical seeing of colours, could be fully explained by physical optics. according to goethe seeing is contemplation, inner contemplation.

goethe thought throughout his life that he was a competent poet but an important scientist. perhaps his breadth of vision can be seen in the fact that the second statement is confirmed from the point of view of contemporary science.

the eye deceives, it has been said, thinking is liberation from illusions. it turns away from what is individual and special. it finds the general, finds order, the laws of nature, of science, of economics, of the state.

this programme is, as we find with all the consequences of false thinking, bankrupt. the altar of reason stood in a cemetery from the beginning.

reason turned into ordo. ordo turned into ideology. ideology turned into domination. domination turned into destruction.

and now we stand around somewhat helplessly with all our knowledge, with all our logic and all our planning.

are we antirational?

we are aware of world-wide movements that are turning to what is within, to emotions and feeling, always in the awareness that rationalism is at an end. there is talk of psi, of the far east, of the female principle.

i cannot accept this. i don't want to send thinking packing. i am going to stick to ratio, to reason, to insight, to the investigation of meaning and purpose, of right and wrong. i stand by the principle that allows me to reflect about such questions and discuss them.

the enlightened view of reason was a torso, cut to size with a view to the disciplines of empirical science.

at the end of this age of enlightenment we find the rationally investigated insight that thinking is not just logical, but seeing. it acquires insights not only through logical operations, like operations with figures. it acquires insights by examining connections, relationships, analogies.

even everyday language gives away the fact that thinking is also a kind of seeing. we speak of insights, of views. philosophy is a view of the world, a world picture. we acquire our own picture of the world. conversely language is not prepared to discriminate against the senses as physically limited authorities susceptible to delusion. according to our language the senses are there to perceive. and so they grasp the truth.

in our most recent cultural history we have tried to get rid of the half of our brain that handles visual thought, our view of things. it is no longer the image, the impression that counts, but the proof.

then came the revolt of the pictures. then came the modern form of communication. and also pictorial inflation. protest was up in arms. there is an uprising: man is a seeing being that sees with his thoughts and thinks in seeing. we must expand the culture of calculation by adding the culture of insight and view.

analogous and digital

anyone who wants to go to rome can find his way along all the roads that lead there in two ways. either he has a travel guide describing the various routes, or a road map. in the first case he is best advised to be like a rally driver and take a prompter, an evangelist with him, in the other case he will be all right on his own. with the travel guide he certainly does not have an overall view, to a certain extent he is driving blind and under instruction, but he can find out exactly where there are old castles and restaurants. with the map he grasps the situation, he is in the picture, he knows the direction, but it is less precise in describing detail.

a digital watch can always be read precisely, to the second. it gives exact numerical values, but i can more easily find out about the landscape of time, whether it is morning or afternoon, too early or too late, from the position of the hands on a watch with a face. the face is like a map, if both hands are at the top it is midday, the small hand on the left means morning or the time after the end of work, the small hand on the right signals the afternoon. with a digital watch i have to translate time value into time landscape. the watch with hands conveys the localization and meaning of the given time more rapidly. but it is less precise.

the digital read-out gives only one value, though of course to as many decimal places as you wish, the analogous display shows a relationship, gives information about a connection. the specatator can see who is the winner of a horse race immediately in the relationship of the horses to each other. the timings for the race are unconnected values and say nothing about the nature of the victory, whether the horse won by a nose or a length.

but there is a group of numbers that has analogous character, that manufactures connections, analogies, and that is the ordinal numbers: first, second, third . . . half a litre of beer is half the biggest beer-mug available. but otherwise numbers are neutral. it is only numerical operations - addition, subtraction, multiplication and division - that create relationships and connections, and thus analogies. one divided by two is a half, produces two halves, produces an ordered relationship.

analogous communication creates insights because it is coupled with sensory perception, particularly with seeing. its scientific dimension is geometry, the mathematics of positions, in contrast with the mathematics of sizes. there is a close relationship between visual perception and thinking, which is analogous seeing. imagine a simple experiment: a motorist is blindfolded and his route is simply explained by a passenger, that is, in words, with the sizes of things, angles and speeds. as soon as the frame of reference is withdrawn he is helpless.

napoleon could never have won his battles if he had not seen the situation as a frame of reference from the top of a hill.

this kind of thinking requires a qualitative response to reality. quality is only another word for relationship, analogy. where there are relationships there is comparison, evalution, quality. digital perception is very probably more precise, but has no element of evaluation. if napoleon counts 200 enemy horses, this only becomes an evaluation when he compares this figure with the number of horses he has himself.

but napoleon does not actually have to begin to count. the exact figure is not important. he knows roughly how many horses he has and compares this with the appearance of the opposing cavalry. he quickly has what he needs: a comparison.

napoleon could also order an adjutant to count his own and the enemy's horses and calculate the ratio. this would produce a precise value, though precision is probably unimportant here. but it may emerge that qualitative statements can be made through counting, through a quantitative investigation.

this provides an important key to understanding modern communication techniques. the first electronic computers were analogous computers, modern ones are digital.

speed can be ignored in electrical processes. as a consequence of this the victory of the digital computer was inevitable. their detours, their primitive processes, their simplified numerical system do not matter. as they work at the speed of light they are always first with their result, never mind the roundabout route they take to achieve it.

this victory is so enormous that a digital age seems to have dawned. people are putting their old watches away in a drawer and buying digital watches that gain or lose less then a minute a year. perhaps the victory would not have been so impressive without two other pre-conditions: the irresistible progress of bureaucracy and the success of statistics. electronic computers found their first fodder in statistics, and their clients in bureaucracy. now they are in their element. additionally they have enormous storage capacity. they hold massive quantities of data, accessible at any time.

we are already incapable of extricating ourselves from the constraints of the digital method. the change in our culture, in our behaviour, in our understanding of the world is impressive. almost everyone already has a second nature, his existence as a quantity of numbers and values. grades from school, biological sizes, figures about family and origin, numbers as an employee, a salary-earner, a motorist, an insurance policy holder, a state citizen, a purchaser.

computers are extremely precise. they can investigate the average height of germans to as many decimal places as you like. but an individual height cannot be calculated from a general average height. in other words, generalization leads away from the individual, generalization is not much use to the concrete. generalization evades reality. generalization tries to dodge the particular.

apparently there is no particular illness either. as testing methods improve they provide increasingly precise values for blood, liver function, cholesterol levels, sugar content, heart rhythm, kidney function . . . whether illness might possibly not be a case open to objectification but has biographical origins that can only be expressed in appropriate values is a question that is not even asked.

indeed it is no longer impossible that digital technology is making man into an increasingly digital being.

at the same time we are discovering more clearly than ever before that man has a new particularity: he is not the much-mentioned thinking being, but a being who thinks analogously. this time it is not epistemological considerations that make this clear, but a new technological field. engineers force us to insights about particular human nature. according to this it would be no longer admissible to divide mind and body, that thinking would be seen as a mental activity and cognition as physical. man thinks with the means of perception, and he perceives with the assistance of thought. his thinking is analogous thinking, seeing thinking. cognition and thinking may be separated conceptually, in fact we are dealing with two aspects of one and the same process.

this unity becomes very clear if perception is disturbed. if our organs of perception are deceived, the brain introduces corrective procedures that recreate the balance between nerve centres and receptors. when the electric light is switched on in the evening we should perceive a white table as yellow, because the light from the bulb is yellowish. but the brain knows that the table is white. consequently the brain causes the cones of the eye to produce a blue dye, almost a blue filter, that makes white back into white.

we think in pictures. picture is understood here not as a painted picture but as a frame with various contents that are perceptible and comparable simultaneously, and thus open to assessment. thus maps too should be seen as pictures, and also our scraps of memory, our imaginings, our dreams. the crucial factor is the perception of various contents that can be compared, that create an analogy, alongside each other. clearly our freedom lies in the possibility of comparing and assessing. a motorist travelling with a travel guide and a description of the route is not free, but someone who can find his own way from a map certainly is - even if it is the same route suggested by the travel guide.

information received from the travel guide's route description could be called linear, one thing follows on from another. there is only a sense of connection when everything is over and done with, at the end. the map, the picture, makes everything available at once. an overall view, a grasp of connections is possible from the beginning. the process of perception is two-dimensional.

it was not until the 20th century that we again discovered that there is a visual language. after the enlightenment and the evaluation of reason appropriate to it, a writing and thinking culture predominated that even knotted the sentences of novels into analytical snakes. it needs similar concentration to read goethe's *wilhelm meister* to that required for kant's critque of pure reason. in the mean time we have learned to read signs, symbols, figures, colours, forms, structures, pictures. national languages are only of limited validity today in communicating the current content of the world. new sign languages in transport, tourism, science have developed. we find it more difficult to judge a position than to mull over thoughts.

now what would happen if we reached the insight that thinking in pictures and the associated visual language had a higher human value than analytical perception and its appropriate mode of expression? what if we were to reach the conviction that human life is not grounded in precision, but in the grasping of connections, facts, relationships, links, analogies? certainly our technical civilization is built on exactness and precision. is our moral, political and cultural existence determined by this as well?

an alternative of this kind is meaningless. thinking in pictures is full of analytical conclusions as well, and even the most scientific text is based on imaginings, landscapes. we are not talking about an alternative but a facesaving exercise.

einstein said about his thinking methods: "words or language, written or spoken, seem to play no part at all in the mechanism of my thought processes. the psychological basic elements of thinking are certain signs and more or less clear pictures that can be reproduced and constructed at will."

if einstein says that it is probably not unreasonable to suggest that humanity could be lost if thinking in pictures is no longer in demand, and atrophies.

however, the meaning of position cognition is not entirely random. it corresponds with the increasing importance of the concept of structure, both in science and technology and in aesthetics. objects have largely been replaced by complexes, houses by blocks, action lines by networks, units of measurement by grids, appliances by systems and form by structure.

human existence today is about grasping complexities, assessing classification, mastering interconnections, recognizing designations.

the crisis in scientific, analytical, logically compelling thinking, the crisis of scientism is a crisis of spot precision. what is truth? the insight is growing that it cannot be acquired through increasing stringency in making precise the agreement between reality and copy. truth emerges from correct linking of meanings in a context.

technology may be forced to extremes of precision, but man needs a sense of proportion. his existence, his subjectivity and his person are built on assessment. he is no longer an integrated natural being but a cultural being inclined to critical alternatives: he finds his position in comparison, in comparison with traditions, in comparison with other systems, in comparison with other people. he is an analogous and not a digital being.

now we do not only have visual thinking for the perception of facts, as a receptive faculty. there are also visual statements as creative language, as sign-settings. since the twenties traffic on the roads has been controlled almost exclusively by visual language, by pictograms. they are equally comprehensible in all languages.

our consumer attitude, whether for good or bad, is primarily determined by the language of advertising, and above all by the language of images. holiday destinations, products, standards of behaviour are conveyed pictorially, often in a consciously staged pictorial presentation. the language of products has been discovered, and the same attention is paid to their appearance as to their technical quality. even architecture is seen as a statement today. its appearance reveals information about structure, about inner function, about the commissioning institution, even about attitude and convictions.

our clothes are more than ever social communication. even hairstyle is a position today, a mental demonstration. after the baroque period, when class and hierarchy were manifested in costume and decoration, the french revolution energetically got rid of plaits, buckles, studs and braids. equality of men led to equality of clothing. only women were permitted to be attractive through choice of fabric and cut.

today women dress like men and men like women, precisely as a social demonstration. the revolt against the ironed crease symbolizes the revolt against class and authority. the way in which hair falls is a manifestation of thought.

afterword

this article was written in 1978. it was published in the same year in circular and the following year in the theologische *quartalshefte*.

it was written under the impression that the concept of thinking is still too summary for our intellectual capability and deserves to be more strongly differentiated. phenomenology introduced an important distinction by distinguishing between understanding and cognition, following the distinction between mind and reason. understanding is the attempt to grasp a thing as a whole, cognition means the collection of perceptual data. hermeneutics extended the concept of thinking by adding an understanding listening, taking in. cognition of a thing means opening oneself up to it and allowing oneself to be permeated by it.

now is thinking speaking, or is it seeing? do we think in sentences or pictures? is it an alegebraic or a geometrical process?

i addressed this question in 1959 in a lecture at the hochschule für gestaltung in ulm. it was delivered at a dons' colloquium, and i tried to understand seeing not just as sensory perception but as inner seeing, involved in the process of drawing conclusions and definition.

i was criticized. at that time thinking was still understood as an "intellectual" activity participating more in a transcendental realm of the true and the good, or as a logical-mathematical operation. even the notions of imagination and *anschauung* could have provoked a little resistance, as they came from the field of the visual.

the 19th century was not a visual century, and cultural awareness was carried by history and literature. it was not until the beginning of this century that the first posters appeared, and film and illustrated papers opened up our awareness of the large part played by picturers in humane culture. the russian revolution of 1917 was already an act of cultural agitation. and wittgenstein noted at the time: understanding a set of facts means making a picture of it for oneself.

in the mean time the subject has become topical. the development of cybernetics and computer technology limited itself to digital thinking and has taken up an exclusive all-round defensive position in the sphere of thought. the question of what is thinking as well as this became compelling. at the same time information theory made a terminological contribution through the distinction between digital and analogous.

the notion of "visual thinking" occurs for the first time as far as i am aware in the work of john c. eccles, who won the nobel prize for his brain research. he used the notion in his 1977/78 lectures at the university of edinburgh. here he drew on research by sperry and levy-agresti, who had localized linguistic-logically orientated thinking in both halves of the human brain through their research on the halves of the brain in 1973 and 1974.

i used the concepts analogous and digital for these different forms of thinking in an academic colloquium in 1978. this took the thinking of the 1959 lecture further. the concepts come from electronic technology and have become common property.

in his book *mind and nature* the british anthropologist and biologist gregory bateson arrived at a similar distinction between analogous and digital thought processes, and pointed out that even the fathers of cybernetics asked themselves whether the brain was an analogous or a digital mechanism. it seems all the more justifiable to apply these concepts not just neurologically, but to make them refer much more to thought itself.

universals and capitals

1
ockham gave us a new view of the world. the ideas that apparently determined things lived a world beyond ours and stood above matter as mind. this dominance of ideas, of the general over the particular, was brought to an end by ockham. he recognized: the ideas are in our heads. we need them in the form of names, concepts and logical thinking.

after this insight man could stop seeing the world as an incarnation of a given truth, goodness and beauty. he had to make a mental effort to find out how and why something had become as it was. this was a rejection of the whole of the ancient and early medieval way of thinking. classicism was dead, and with it the eternal values that had hovered over everything from the beginning of time.

things became a product of development and an arrangement in their environment. they were determined by the balance of their behaviour, not by the spiritual realities of the beyond.

god was not dead for ockham. but he did not know a god who had thought and created everything from the beginning. god was a god of reality, of history, of the history of man and the history of nature.

if ockham were to come back today he would be astonished to see how little his thinking has achieved. certainly science went completely his way, indeed it only became possible because thinking orientated itself by the concrete. but our intellectual culture is more than ever determined by belief in the eternal verities.

today a house can no longer be a system for living in, an optimization point for the best kind of living. a house is part of the eternal house. postmodern architects are looking for the eternal house, for eternal beauty, for the eternal column, the eternal portal. classical thinking is not dead. architecture strives for higher things, for more beautiful things, is style, is a manifestation of eternal truth, goodness and beauty. we still seek the temple, it is just that the materials have changed. today we build in glass, steel and marble. architecture is art. as an artist the architect is closest to the eternal creator, who made everything.

ockham would be amazed how few architects there still are who devote themselves to living, to the people who live in their houses, to the development of better forms for working and living, to the house as a utensil, and to viable cities.

a post-modern society that lives on prestige forgets the development of architecture from concern with the matter in hand. architecture has to be form, to have style.

2

our language has a structure that grew historically, it is a cultural product. it grew from sentence structure and the hierarchy of words. the meaning of words was not always the same. today our key word is the noun, in german we even give it the distinction of beginning with letters from an ancient script, roman capital letters. until the renaissance and baroque period there was only one script, the one we call lower case today. but then nouns started to be decorated with the letters the ancient romans used, even if this meant recourse to a script that was less legible. the modern view was that it was more beautiful, and it came from rediscovered classical antiquity.

anyone who suspects a link with political and social development here is right. the script follows the development towards princely absolutism. from now on the world is to be ruled from above. the all-embracing state replaces autonomous cities. to this end everything that protected and sustained this state had to be favoured and enhanced: god, the church, kings, ministries, all the institutions of the state. their names were decorated with the capital letters of a script steeped in culture, and so were the things that emerged from such institutions, rules, laws, ordinances, dispositions, decrees. this has remained the case until the present day.

if something is ordered, that is an order, if something is withdrawn, that is a withdrawal, if you want to promote someone, that is a promotion.

today our german language has so many nouns that it is starting to become paralyzed, and it is slowly becoming clear that actually it is not nouns that are our key words, but verbs.

verbs describe what is happening, what is emerging, flowing, active, effective. verbs represent the world as a dynamic sequence. working is something different from, something more actual than "work". loving is something different from, something more actual than "love". love is the frozen, the solidified condition of what we call loving. the state is the frozen, petrified condition of that which it is supposed to administer.

and so an age that perceives itself as moving and moved should make the verb the key word. we no longer tolerate the world as a static solidification of power. for this reason distinctions are solidifications of language, capital letters are wrong. we ought to distinguish verbs, or at least stop distinguishing nouns.

ockham would agree with that without reservation. he dethroned the so-called universals, the nouns of thinking.

3

wittgenstein originally intended to find and develop a definite form of logic, by which all sentences could be identified as true or false. he wanted to solve all problems of philosophy this way.

he discovered that this could not be done. he saw that he was attached to a certain extent to a classical model of understanding the world according to which there was a superordinate general validity.

but language is not final. words refuse to be fixed, and so do the rules of language. language is in a state of flux. a word that has a positive meaning today can have a negative one tomorrow. thus today the word "state" is becoming ambivalent, contradictory, although yesterday it sounded inviolably positive. even when priests talk of "love" we begin to doubt whether they know what it is.

how does language copy reality? as static symmetry or fluctuatingly in sporadic transformations? does language live on observation, or is it a product of eternal validity?

if one reads the writings of wittgenstein one has the impression that he had books by ockham on his bedside table, and that ockham gave him the courage to go on.

wittgenstein then found out that language is like sport. language has rules that change according to the course of the game. wittgenstein recommended to philosophers that they play language games. because he was convinced that the meaning of language was its use. truth arises from use.

truth develops from creative use, architecture develops from creative use, modernism is creative use.

57

many people think that a house with a flat roof is modern. in that case mies van der rohe would be modern. then modernism would be the application of superordinated, general, universal forms. this is how the bauhaus saw it as well, with its doctrine of square, circle and triangle.

is mies van der rohe modern? isn't he really a classicist? a classicist with new materials, but still an architect of universal validity?

he was not looking for brilliant solutions for trivial things like living and work, he found appearances for representing the valid and great. he built in the same way that st. thomas aquinas wrote his philosophy. he built universals, something actually valid.

in comparison with this ockham would be the patron of the functionalists. everything in the world is a case. everything is a response to a situation. nothing is a quotation. nature does not repeat itself, man is different tomorrow from today, the world is different tomorrow from today. how will it be? creative use shows this. what is great, once classicism, does not tell us how it will be.

the modern thing is to think non-classically, to forget universals (and let the capital letters die out).

4

in the traditional sense, graphics is the attempt to give publications artistic value. and hence the concept: applied art.

this is not the case in rotis. here graphics means optimized communication. in other words, there are no categories of art, there are categories of communication. no attempt is made to elevate the profane, to enhance its value, by using something loftier, namely art. it is much more that an attempt is made to take communication so seriously and to process it in such a way that it becomes art itself. in rotis art is the form in which what is correct appears.

that is a fundamental distinction. for plato, our world was participation in something higher, participation in the ideal. the mind is above. it is different for ockham. mind is not above, it is a method of interpreting what is given, of understanding something and making it understandable. mind is confrontation with the thing itself.

there is no wonder that ockham is seen as an occasional guest in rotis.

in rotis there is not only no prescribed art. there is also no aesthetics as such. it is within the matter in hand and wants to be brought out. there is no possibility of making a statement about the aesthetics of tomorrow.

the spirit of the age is not found in rotis. the age has no spirit. there are no strings on which the figures of the age are made to dance like marionettes in a play. the age is the sum of the activities and endeavours that individuals develop in their environment.

for this reason there is no superordinated style in rotis, unless it is considered style to make what is correct appear. but that is more of a method. in rotis we reflect about what we are doing.

just as plato's ideas and the universals of st. thomas aquinas have disappeared from the philosophy of ockham, art has disappeared in the case of those people who declare life itself, becoming and doing, the world as it is, to be the sphere of creative making. the profane and higher things no longer exist, there is no elevated german any more. on the contrary, anyone who tries to speak educated, refined german is speaking incorrect german.

what is communication? what we understand. what is mind? what we see and understand.

to optimize both you need a daily design draft. there can be no recourse to higher things. and that also means that you need the design draft for the everyday.

buridan and peirce

a concept is not a portrayal of a thing or a set of facts. the word circle is not round. and in french it would look quite different from the way it looks in german, the french word for circle is cercle, the german, kreis.

to this extent one can say that if we portray reality in concepts we are not actually portraying, but only referring. the sign for circle is a linguistic-phonetic shorthand symbol that is determined by various conventions in various languages.

but are concepts the material of our thinking and is associative speaking, the statement sentence, the portrayal of a fact? many philosophies are based on this.

one of the first people to have thought differently about this is buridan, the most recent is peirce.

buridan, moving on directly from ockham, did not see thinking so much as working with language as comparing pictures and notions. ockham makes the great step from ancient to modern by understanding thinking as thinking about the content of statements and no longer as thinking about external orders of being. for this reason thinking is not cut off from the outside, words refer to things and states of affairs, but only refer. they represent the actual. this again only in the form of language, in associative form, by means of which words are turned into sentences.

when buridan places notions alongside words as well and handles relationships like geometrical connections, then as far as the ancient world is concerned, which scholasticism was trapped in as well, he is making a similar step of internalization and operational handling as ockham had done with language.

under scholasticism pictures were involved in the perception process, though only in the form of perceiving sensory impressions. the intellect then had to derive from these perception-pictures the abstract characteristics that made the substance of the real object stand out. there was thus a pressure towards the general, towards the ordering of things and being, that ultimately corresponded with the creator's ideas. this means that understanding is abstractly stripping the concrete image to reach the core of the statement.

this is how plato, aristotle and st. thomas aquinas saw it.

for buridan the picture is starting point for a notion that is more than a portrayal. for him thinking is comparing notions, developing entanglements of connections, preparing models. terministic nominalism becomes conceptual, and as the former becomes the basis of modern science, the latter opens up thinking space for modern technology as it is now developing. the picture as a notion, as intellectual architecture in the movement process of thinking, is something different in comparing and evaluating from the empirical picture of a passive reality. intellect develops its constructive design in notions. for buridan the picture is no longer the painter's copy, but the designer's, the architect's, the planner's notional picture. the notion then has sign character, no longer stands for external states of affairs, but moves into perspective.

for peirce this notion becomes a "mental picture" in contrast with the real picture. he calls this mental picture an "icon" and says that it exists only in the consciousness. and even more: it is possible to think only with such pictures. he insists that we think in icons and that abstract statements are worthless in thinking if they don't help us to make diagrams. for peirce icons are no longer manifestations of the real, graphs, diagrams, reference fields with curves belong here as well and the spatial organization of statements. the objects of thought are figuration and proportioning of consciousness-content, are formal and structural configurations. even when we write down an algebraic equation we raise a field of figurative references to the status of a picture and thus create the possibility of reading it at a glance. a flow chart or a development curve gives our thinking another field of reality that ancient and medieval philosophy as good as excluded, the world of emergence and decay, the world of processes, the world in time, the world of history, the world of flux. this also raises the verb to the rank in philosophy that is has in everyday speech. the process-like element of reality is opened up for thinking, and also the process-like element of culture.

in places where it runs off into definitions and chains of proof, thinking also occurs in figurations, is accompanied by ordering design that feeds on a culture of forms, graphs, structures, proportions and perspectives. the icon does not only capture objects, but also conditions. "what a notion to believe that you could think of movement without a picture of something moving!" admittedly this does not means that

61

we would think in illustrative pictures. perception only takes place when the illustration-picture becomes a sign, reveals its structure, when the icon becomes a characterizing sign.

there is also a reciprocal process to this in man. in dreams the visual structures of thinking and the icons dissolve as abstractions and move back into the realm of illustration.

reading scores

recent research suggests that johann sebastian bach could read a score according to visual criteria. he saw it as a picture and corrected it like a draughtsman, according to its graphic structure. music seemed like a picture to him, and he created his music by making graphic notations.

as such, a written note is a sign for the pitch and duration of a tone, and as such notes are read one after the other, as the instrument in question has to play them, or one above the other when several instruments together are playing different notes. notes are digital values. but you can read a tune as a line like the contours of a mountain range. it produces an analogous band. and a chord too can be read not in values but as a stacked picture. then one does not recognize the notes of which it consists, but its overall sound, its sound picture.

quite obviously bach did not read notes as linear or horizontal chains, as one reads language in a linear fashion, but as interconnections and networks, as shapes, as graphic relation-fields. instead of listing spring flowers he captured a spring meadow and instead of listing autumn flowers, digitalizing them, he saw an autumn meadow.

glenn gould said something similar about himself. he had first of all to translate music into a spatial-visual notion, he had to see how it ran and interconnected to be able to play it.

this did not mean that he could avoid the analytical process. only when he had put it together note by note, when he had put stone on top of stone did the house come into being, the space, the sound space, the shape and the idea.

even when we are manipulating figures we do this with the assistance of spaces, landscapes and figurations. when adding up a bill we move in a ladder that leads through different areas. and every number that we add is like a parcel that we pile on top of other parcels. there are light and dark places in the ladder of figures, good and bad figures. the leap to the next unit of ten is like a leap over a frontier. many numbers are pleasant, others are repugnant, some are handled by trickery.

hearing and counting, reading and calculating, smelling and feeling are always connected with ideas, with brightnesses, with spaces, with structures, with analogies and landscapes. in this context listening to music is particularly complex. often four, five, six lines of notes are overlayered and interpenetrate, in bach even with the highest degree of autonomy and individuality.

even a football match with twenty-two players and twenty-two sequences of movement can be "seen". it cannot be analysed.

honourable burial for descartes

the modern age began with the killing of phenomena. the gravity that causes apples and raindrops to fall to the ground creates a phenomenon, the fall. the fall of light things, the fall of heavy things. every fall is an event.
galilei was not interested in this fall. he was not interested in the phenomenon, but in the way it could be copied in a set of figures. for him the phenomenon was only significant to the extent that it provided figures, rows of figures that revealed conformity with a natural law.
for this there were two categories of number series, one for time, the duration of a free fall, and one for the distance that an object covers in falling. a third category that seemed to suggest itself he could forget: the weight of the falling objects. contrary to all appearances, contrary to our perception of the phenomenon, snow falls as quickly as an apple, provided there is no air resistance. there was of course gravity, or the attraction of the earth, but that was a constant, with the same value for each and every thing.
the values that galilei arrived at for distance and time in free fall showed a constant interrelationship, a conformity with natural law. he captured them in a formula: $s = 1/2 g \cdot t^2$. this means that the distance in free fall is equal to half gravity x time squared. the scientific age had begun, the age of investigating natural laws.
phenomena were removed from the field of view, they disappeared.
of course there is no such thing as free fall as such. there is always something falling, an apple, snow, a girl. fall only exists concretely, in the phenomenon. and there every fall is different. the wind plays a part, air resistance, the pull of the moon, the various values for earth attraction, in fact even molecular movement in the falling object. if there were a moment when all the molecules were moving in the same direction a brick could fall upwards. no fall is like another, each is a phenomenon.
none of this interested galilei. he was interested in falling as such, something that does not exist. he was interested in copying the fall in a set of figures. this made it possible to calculate how something falls and the direction in which it falls.

65

this was the birth of technology. from now on the flight of shells could be calculated, then bombs, and then rockets. from now on there was technology without values, that could and might do everything because it was no longer bound by phenomena. technology was a method of doing everything that was possible, that could be calculated, without reliance on phenomena, their perception and their assessment. anything that fell now, be it apple, snow or shell, fell as a result of natural laws, within a framework of natural laws, through the legitimation of natural laws.

descartes went a step further. he was not so much concerned with nature and its laws. he was concerned to improve the projection quality of numerical values. how can the values investigated and their relationships best be presented? to this end he suggested so-called systems of co-ordinates with a vertical and a horizontal axis.

to represent the curve of a projectile, time was entered on the horizontal axis and distance on the vertical. the projectile started at the point of intersection of the axes, where the value for time and distance was zero, rose in the direction of the time axis and the distance axis, but then fell back to a zero value for time at precisely the point at which the distance of the flight came to an end.

this was a two-dimensional process, every point on the curve of the projectile had exact numerical value, projected vertically on the time and distance axis. each axis was a measuring rod with precise values. the flight of the shell could now be translated into an arithmetical equation. the curve itself became uninteresting. the significant fact was that the curve became calculable, no longer related to illustration, but to arithmetical operations. the image of the phenomenon, the curve, disappeared as well, what remained was the arithmetical operation. the image, the illustration, the geometrical curve were lost with the phenomenon as well.

the digital age had begun. even pascal, a contemporary of descartes, who expressed reservations about abstract reason, was involved in building the first calculating machines.

the world shrunk into a series of arithmetical operations. technology developed to the extent that it was an arithmetical procedure, and science withdrew from observation and calculation into arithmetical processes.

the phenomenon had been killed, but the image disappeared as well. reality was reduced to calculable conformity with natural law.

of course this has something to do with the collapse of our civilization. wars arising from madness break out to plague us, social techniques that despise human beings smother individuality, technical progress is unrecognizable when it suffocates in its own rubbish. a better world is produced as a by-product of the destruction of nature and we breed new human beings while abandoning their personality, morality and dignity. utimately there could be only a person without an ego left who is capable of sustaining the dynamic, the eternal growth of digital production. but man is not a digital creature, and because he is not, a digitalized civilization could drum him out of position and authority, until there is only one living creature left, one that digital civilization keeps alive at the point where it cannot quite control everything itself.

a simple proof. we show someone three squares. we ask him what it is, what it could mean.

some guess tiles, some squares of chocolate, some windows. some simply say: three squares. which is not wrong.

we show him a second drawing. we ask him what is is, and promptly get the answer: a cube.

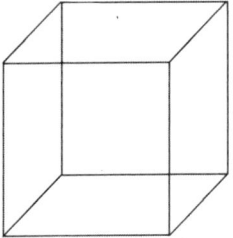

both drawings show the same thing. the top example is a drawing of a cube by the cartesian method, as top view, side view and front view. this drawing makes it possible to define the cube exactly, and give measurements for each side. in the lower example the side view degenerates to a trapezium. and a cube does not have a side like a trapezium. the drawing is correct, but not true. nevertheless the lower drawing immediately shows what we are dealing with. the second drawing is analogous, gives a clear portrayal of the object. it is clear to everyone, europeans and asiatics, schoolchildren and grownups, workers and scientists, and so it is right, even though it is not true.

the top drawing with three views of the cube is read differently by everybody. the portrayal is wrong, but the values that define a cube are reproduced in unadulterated form. you can measure every side from this drawing. you can build cubes from this drawing. but you can't understand them. and it is not only cubes that are built by this method. houses are built like this, appliances and machines.

descartes had an ambition to reproduce things in their truth. he succeeded in the sense that now every technician could produce an object precisely, in accordance with the numerical values given in a three-dimensional projection. without this drawing technique and without the projection of threedimensional objects on three planes of co-ordinates there would not have been any modern technology. it would not have been possible to manufacture precisely turned crankshafts, cannon muzzles or car cylinders. and yet this drawing is still more misleading than a help. analogous drawing shows what it is all about. it shows a phenomenon and thus makes it comprehensible to human culture, which is an analogous culture, and one of correct pictures.

with descartes, with digitalization in co-ordinate systems, man disappears from civilization, the individual and the subject disappear, because they can no longer take part in history and development. a language is now spoken that that can probably be understood by a mathematician and an engineer, a statistician and an entrepreneur, as a meta-language of their professions, but which remains generally unintelligible. for man is an analogous and not a digital being, even if he can make use of digital technology.

man with his way of seeing and thinking disappears from the scene. technology and science develop without human involvement and also without its assessment and control.

this is the only way in which it is possible to understand that the world of today is turning itself inside out, twisting and turning, to the point of turning progress into annihilation. we can no longer follow what is happening around us because as living beings we were programmed in analogous language. our mind thinks with our eyes. thinking and seeing are one and the same thing. when the mind thinks alone, when it digitalizes, we lose our view of the world. we do not have analogies any more, no more comparisons. only in exceptional cases, for instance when the new technologies of war compel us to creep into cellars, does our questioning push through the back door and out into civilization to ask for enlightenment. we do not even allow ourselves to suspect that we live in a world that has gone wrong, in which phenomena no longer count, and pictures of them are not available as aids to understanding either.

actually descartes dug his own grave. he wanted the truth. and he got it, in so far as it is available in numbers. but he lost the world as a world. everything happens as if in a secret technology with a secret language. we sink or swim by this technology that is so difficult for us to control. it determines our way of life and the aims of our lives. but what we really perceive, the things that surround us, work and pleasure, love and hate, city and country, good and evil, value and non-value, war and peace, the whole of the world open to experience, that we can see but also understand, is not precise, and therefore second-rate. it can be neglected.

and so we are outside. unless we turn things round. we stand by a form of thought that is particular to man. and so we should admit to ourselves: the precise world is the false one.

digitalization proclaims the general as such. the self is always a phenomenon, an individual one. but only the self has a point of view.

the self is the central point of the world. it is the axis of the hands that show the points of the compass, give us orientation. positions and values can only be derived from the self. the world is an interplay of subjects. the statistical average value of their behaviour is always general. but only the general is calculable, open to digitalization. population policies can only be carried out by someone who has liberated the population from the self. military strategies can only be developed by someone who has freed the army of selves. only then can they be counted and used operationally. a citizens' rights movement, a fight for freedom, an uprising, a revolt cannot be accommodated in this numbers game. they thrive on the power of individuality.

the world of the individual is the world of culture. culture is the appearance of singularity, of the individual position, the individual offer. but it cannot be measured.

but the world is measured, nature is measured, the economy is measured, politics are measured. and anyone who measures comes up with values, often large ones, but always general ones: the fatherland, freedom, humanity. and the more we measure the more we digitalize, the more we generalize and fall into generalities the higher the abstract values become, right up to the religion of reason and the salvation message of enlightenment. it brings us a new humanity without human beings, belief in all that without a view of the individual.

the criterion of generality is the balance, the confirmation of the formula.

and yet today even statistics breathe the breath of terror. how many woods are sick, how many species are becoming extinct, how many people are dying of new diseases, these insights do not tell us of the individual fate, but the results of the test. let us recognize the achievement of descartes and the digitalized modern age. but how does it help us to know what percentage of nature is destroyed when it is the foot of each individual driver on the accelerator that is causing it.

we must change our point of view. we must know that we not only see and think. we must know that we see and think in different ways. our thinking is not an apparatus, a disposition derived from nature. it is an instrument, a cultural instrument, with various tools and techniques. we must learn to understand methods of thinking as causes for the way we see the world.

and in doing this we have reason no longer to see galilei's counting method and descartes' digitalizing method as the method as such, the method of the mind as such, the method of truth as such. these methods are discredited.

if precision were the meaning of life then these methods might be followed. life was not out for precision, but for development and harmony. to this extent our mind's inclination to precision is very probably significant, but only a means of achieving correlation between ourselves and our environment.

precision is a secondary characteristic of our cosmos, of our nature, which is always an event and always developing. we have descartes to thank for the fact that we were able to fathom the laws of nature. but their starting point is always the event.

we must learn to discover events again, to describe them. then we will perhaps rediscover the subject, ourselves.

but if we want to discover phenomena again, want to discover individuals, we must place correct thinking in its true light vis-à-vis true thinking.

the true world is relative, because it is abstract, general, indeed true. the real world is the world of phenomena. understanding it means looking and listening, not knowing in advance what is going to happen.

science and technology are artificial limbs, useful, but artificial. they only show what is general, not the event. but the world, life, history are made up of events. there is not a single law that tells me what will happen tomorrow. because a law is only an approximate picture of what happened as an event. only what actually happens, what becomes an event, creates natural law. only the phenomenon is the world.

describing a phenomenon as present is possibly more important than explaining it from the past. in each case it is individual, concrete, not general.

the behaviour of galilei, his supra-historical opportunity in the face of the church's claim to truth was itself a fall. as yet there are no rules for this fall. and yet in fact galilei's behaviour is more significant for us today than his scientific achievement. (An additional fact is that scientific investigation of free fall is also attributed to nicolaus von oresme, who lived two hundred years earlier.) galiei is himself a fall. an event.

and even if we ask in the case of descartes why he turned western philosophy back to platonic antiquity we do not find any assistance in general laws. descartes was in fact an accident and not so much a fall. he never perceived that since william of ockham western philosophy had distanced itself from the problems of the general. because of the compulsory scholastic education of his youth he took refuge in the ancient rather than the modern and became more idealistic than plato himself.

descartes too is a fall. a fateful one, in fact. it would be wrong to bürden him with everything that has emerged from his arithmetical generalizations. the world of growth rates, interest, yield, average values, summation equations, key facts, invoices, quotients, trends and all the other numerical revelations you might think of is too shabby to be laid directly at descartes' door. and it was also a heroic deed to entrust statements about the world to a system of co-ordinates rather than statements from the old or new testament.

but we should neverthless allow descartes to pass to his eternal rest. he still lives on. this age rests upon his shoulders. in the mean time he deserves a burial, an honourable one.

we can allow ourselves to be generous because we know that what he wanted was wrong. the generalizations captured by exact science are the result of calculations. but the one thing the world is not is the result of calculations. and neither is descartes himself. descartes made the general absolute not just philosophically, but quantitively as well, by calculation.

the burial can be honourable so long as we are aware of one thing: he got us into something evil. we understand the world only as a calculation, as a set of laws.

it is not just that nutritional chemists tell us how many proteins and vitamins we should eat, behavioural researchers even know how much aggression can be tolerated as conforming to natural law. everyone prepares statistical presentations according to the cartesian co-ordinate system, and everyone is looking for the quantity formula of optimization.

descartes deserves an honourable burial so long as it is final. the only question is: can we collect up everything we need to bury?

galilei and descartes established truth as a principle as opposed to truth as an institution. the thing counted, not the authority. they set up science and technology against the principles of the church as the guardian of truth. this deserves a great deal of respect, even if everything they did had been wrong.

but at the same time they created a new institution, not of truth any longer but of science and technology. even the modern state is a state by descartes' and galilei's grace. it is now the state and not the church that knows what is the truth. it says what should be promoted scientifically and executed by technology. it knows what is socially relevant, tolerable to the individual and sustainable by the environment.

the religion of handing down through books and testaments has been replaced by the religion of reason, of science, of enlightenment, and its institution is no longer called vatican or council but state.

descartes did not intend the individual detail of this, but as adviser to the queen of sweden he even sacrificed his life to create an institution for the new religion as well.

since then the state has pursued or promoted progressive economics, medicine, educational policy, technology, military strategy, rocket technology and genetic manipulation.

the state, the church of reason, of technology, of science. it does not concern itself only with principles, but also with success. we must bury descartes quickly, and still honourably, before his repercussions overtake him.

the state is the institution of the general, of general welfare, of reason, of law, of the beautiful, true and good. but who is interested in the general if we are concerned with the concrete? and we are increasingly concerned with the concrete.

and additionally, anyone who has his eye on truth as truth, the good as good and general welfare as general welfare, is guilty of excessive bureaucratization, excessive generalization, running things down, twisting and officializing the thing into its opposite. the individual becomes a tiny cog in the general, in the progress of science and technology.

design and philosophy

1
design, like advertising, is a 20th century invention, and came into being in parallel with industrial production. today it is a central component of the phenomenon known as "lifestyle", a colour- and shape-happy behavioural manifestation of post-industrial leisure society. people live in brands and models. the modern manufacturer knows that the modern subject does not only identify with brands and shapes, but presents himself in them as a second body.

design, before it became a predominantly economic quantity, was a cultural movement aiming to overcome classical bourgeois style fixated on historical styles. it still has a cultural as well as an economic dimension today. if the question posed by culture once was how man can set himself up as a human being in a reality prescribed by nature and in a prescribed world, then the question was asked of the world of industrially produced goods of how man can establish himself in a newly-made world of technical artefacts, and perhaps survive and defend himself as well.

design is understood as the manufacture of beautiful things, as aesthetic creation. "good form" is a broad spectrum, both as far as the products are concerned and also in terms of the motivation of what can be called aesthetic. in english design was originally the equivalent of the german "entwurf", suggesting a draft, the development of a new object or a new thing. german also had the concept of "gestaltung", shaping, moulding, fashioning, referring less to the technical aspects of a thing than to its form. for a time we used the word "formgebung", literally formgiving, but this fell into disrepute because it looked as though a new, external form was simply being foisted upon objects. in fact this completely fits most contemporary processes concerned with form: a "gestalt", a shape or form is foisted upon things. they are made to conform to a style, stylized. recently the term styling has also been introduced for this, in german as well.

the fact that object and form are separated when considering something, in other words the form is seen as variable, alterable at will according to the spirit of the times and media taste, corresponds to a bourgeois view of culture according to which the world is divided into mind and matter, form and

75

technology, style and purpose, appearance and substance. design has somewhat declined to a modish attitude along these lines recently, something that changes like hairstyle and the length of skirts. designers are cultural hairdressers who apply the styles of art, the tastes of the time to everyday products as well, thus enhancing their marketability, but also promoting the desired aesthetic consumption that is the dream of everyone who thinks in turnover figures. it is only design that can create the throw-away product that is a prerequisite of the modern economy.

the division of form and technology, of design and construction is naturally only an image of a deeper crisis in our civilization, and that is the division of capital and work. it is not the manufacturers who determine the purpose and appearance of a product, but the people who earn money from it.

in this way design degenerates to be a modish scrap of a profit-maximizing society, a fashionable cheap dress for stoking consumption, for children as well, and as a style façade for a post-modern consumer society. there is probably no remedy for this, particularly after governments have discovered that design is an outstanding means for improving the sales opportunites of their economy and increasing the national income. and governments also control the teachers and directors, the curriculum and aims of their design schools. an army of design cretins is brought in who all want to have a share in the blessings that design brings. it is a colour-happy, a form-rich blessing.

but why should the new world be better than the old? the alliance of culture and industry, of culture and power, is as old as the need not only to cover up the greatest crimes of rapacious economics, but to make people forget about them. sometimes they are even successfully reversed, and crime is restyled as a blessing. anyone who promotes culture, science and art is an honourable man, even if his name is carnegie or rockefeller.

the alliance of culture and industry was taken out of service for a time because it was so embarrassing. today it is coming back with a vengeance. the lackey is called design. and both art historians and cultural sociologists, all trained at state colleges, give the whole thing the blessing of objectivity.

but that is only one side. official or officious culture was always wide of the mark. culture develops by addressing the world, not money.

despite all this, design has remained a cultural activity, and its space for reflection is filled with fundamental questions of human existence under the conditions not only of industrial reproduction but of industrial production, in other words of life in a new, largely artificial world.

if the distinction between mind and matter, body and soul, form and content, appearance and thing cannot be sustained for much longer, then the question arises of how all the technical products, tools, appliances, machines, flats, means of transport and instruments of communication have to be made so that man can perceive them as his own.

this is where things start to get exciting. for how can this be contrived?

the story of design in this century is a story of various approaches. this story has not yet been written, but between werkbund and bauhaus, between constructivism and rationalism, between olivetti and braun, between art deco and post-modernism a cultural landscape has emerged in which the real actions are more dramatic than theatre, however well invented. culture is being experienced as a process at a time when culture is being sold.

in this field of confrontation there are confrontations as hard as those between people who question technology about its forms in order to formulate an aesthetic of technology and those who found a rational aesthetic as a primeval geometry of aesthetic appearance intended to form the basis of every shape. should we build houses more according to their structural principles or more according to the codes of crystalline elementary geometry? should we build cars as mobile seating in modern traffic conditions, or as symbols of speed? this is material for a broad and fundamental cultural debate.

a crucial area of this debate is the question: can design restrict itself to products, appliances, plants, machines, houses, cities, or is design a decision about a form of life? is only the product part of design, or what we do with it, how we handle it?

germany was one of the most important scenes of the workers' movement, but the workers were fighting only for more wages and shorter hours. a later addition are the alternative and green parties who do not ask first what our society generates but why it does it. this inevitably leads to conflict with design that only perceives itself as beautiful packaging. the packaging of our food becomes more beautiful the more questionable it is. the one is dependent upon the other. what is design today? what does designing mean? the discussion about design extends even further. it all comes down to the question of whether we can still allow ourselves the luxury of simply recognizing the world, rather than designing it. is our rationalistic culture of knowledge and our scientific morality of neutral objectivity not at an end, a point where annihilation of life is within the realms of the possible and can only be averted by a creative design intervention, a design in the dimension of what is feasible, of manufactured reality, not just of the insight in principle? design is no longer a shaping concept, it moves into the realms of philosophy, of explanations of the world and understanding of the times.

at the moment when an honest design intelligence asks these new questions of design, the discovery is made that philosophy has also broken out of the bastions of rational insight into the world and is asking itself how we create access to a world that is not just an object of cognition.

we must understand our civilization as a self-designed new world. where we do not give in to conformity. we must see modern life as a design. we have to ask about meaning and purpose, function and use in an all-embracing sense, not one that is related to individual products. it is no longer abstract, conceptual truth that is our problem, but correctness, the manufactured correct facts of the matter, living space that has been built. we must move over from thinking to making and learn to think again by making.

2

philosophy has in some cases moved along the path from thinking to making, from speculative thinking to thinking in use, in my opinion some of its rare high spots, in the work of kant and wittgenstein, for example. kant is generally known as the philosopher of pure reason. this false interpretation was fostered above all by the title of his principal work, the *critique* of pure resaon. here kant was concerned to stake out the bounds of reason, to show critically where its limits lie.

he turned against the philosophies of men like descartes, spinoza or leibniz, who thought they had found truth in purely speculative thinking, by analogy with algebra, in the development of pure thinking methods. truth lies in general principles that lie behind things. deducing them is philosophy.

kant contradicts this energetically, but does not follow the english authors of his period, who wanted to see cognition merely as experience of the real, as empirical perception. for kant cognition comes from things, but not from themselves, but from *anschauung*, view, the pictures we have of them. the mind processes these views with its categories. this also sets the limitations of the mind. it can only process what can be viewed, and then again only within the limits of its categories.

kant becomes a victim of his own formulation. the title critique of pure *reason* can be understood in two ways. critique can mean a limiting reprimand, but also appreciation.

looking at it closely, kant is not at all the philosopher of reason, but of *anschauung*, of view. he raises *anschauung* to the plane of philosophical business and only permits reason to operate on this plane in accordance with its categories and principles. kant withdraws the verdict of being inimical to the mind from anschauung, and therefore from the senses. kant was by no means the prussian pietist with a highly developed sense of moral responsibility that people like to paint him. he was by no means offering the world to something higher by belittling worldly, sensual, physical things as opposed to the power of the mind. on the contrary, the mind had to be told that it cannot go beyond what the senses bring in. it is dependent on *anschauung*.

this is more than a concern with technical problems of possible cognition. this evaluation is one way in which life is endowed with meaning. how can we understand ourselves and how do we treat ourselves? this is not just a painful question of culture, of religion and the exercise of power, it is also a painful question of our own intellectual, moral and psychological balance and content or discontent with ourselves.

this rescue of the honour of *anschauung*, of the picture, the ability to project and imagine certainly does not remove the requirement for precise thinking, but destroys reason's claim to total dominance. it can no longer appear with the claim to have a share in the substance of the world with its precise methods. the general insights of the mind can no longer be the mirror of general laws, necessities and truths according to which the world is made. reason cannot be world reason, it is craft in one's own little room and it would be deaf and blind without the harvests of *anschauung*, principally introduced by the eye of man.

kant took over his reservations about arrogant reason from hume. his republican way of thinking comes from rousseau. republicans are concerned to question any authority and to feed the suspicion that a highest principle of reason was only introduced to justify authority as such. the republican uses the individual as his starting point in philosophy as well, makes him part of its laws and exchanges divine reason for a living human being, thinking with body and soul.

but now something peculiar happens. kant had already completed his *critique of pure reason* and his *critique of practical reason*. at the age of 66 he was overtaken by the question of whether *anschauung* and imagination do not come before the judgement of reason, and not just as the process evolves, but also in meaning. what determines our thinking, reason or sensory perception, rational, systematic judgement or aesthetic judgement?

he is guided by an important and new insight in this. kant sees the world as made. it is not something that is, but it is manufactured, both in nature, which is in a state of constant development, and also in technology or culture.

once philosophy was the search for the truth, for a plan behind the world, for its order as the order of a cosmos, an existence. now the question arises: what determines its development, how should it be designed?

in doing this people who manufacture things, technicians, architects, men of letters can work less on a basis of knowledge, as knowledge describes what exists. it works on target notions and teleological judgements. these target notions are predominantly evaluations. they are based on projections that are accompanied by requests, concerns and expectations. and these notions are oriented towards concrete cases, not general knowledge. they relate to what is feasible, and this is always concrete and always individual. purpose comes before general knowledge. and it is always the concrete that is suited to a purpose. it is projected at a meaning, a general insight, but an insight into what has to be made, what has to be designed. that requires constructive imagination that does not stop at the object as such, but relates it in imagination to goals, evaluations, constellations. the mind is decisively involved in this "figurative synthesis", but it is carried by evaluating sensory perception.

at the age of forty kant had paid marginal attention to aesthetics. a summer stay in the country induced him to "observations on the feeling of the beautiful and sublime". but aesthetics seemed unsusceptible to scientific-rational intervention. even at the age of sixty kant did not believe that aesthetic judgement could have anything to do with philosophy.

kant then discovered that the world is not only reasonable, but functional, that it is not only its objective truth that is of importance, but also its meaning. at the age of almost seventy he wrote the *critique of judgement*.

if our life forms are determined by functionality, if the mind is not sufficient for correct doing, then a new kind of thinking and judging is necessary. the word "urteilskraft" (power of judgement) remains close to mind and reason. here judgement takes place primarily, while in reality we are dealing with sensory perception. "sensory perception as a principle of explanation" would have been a title to signal a turning back. imagination is mentioned in the text itself, the title retains the discipline of rationality.

in this matter kant remains open, rigorous and bold. anschauung, sensual judgement, aesthetic harmony are no longer the other, excluded area of thinking, as classical rationalism asserted until the present day. they are much more the actual organ of a *weltanschauung*. truth becomes sensory truth. meaning is revealed via sensory perception. the world becomes one of perspectives. the criterion is functionality that withdraws from generalization and is produced in acting and doing, in manufacture.

kant arrives at the unusual insight that sensory perception is also a form of cognition, not just thinking in the categories of reason. he is guided by a new view of nature. her creatures do not just move themselves, but organize themselves. nature is self-organization. but self-organization also requires insight, cognition.

and so there is a broad field of cognition that is not, unlike the case of man, determined by the ability to form concepts and combine these to draw conclusions. there is a cognition without concepts, without the organs of understanding and reason, which guarantees that animals behave in their own interest, reproduce themselves, and enter into a balance of conservation with their environment, form themselves into communities and maintain the equilibrium of nature. their insight is concrete, relates to individual facts and situations, they do not generalize, but it is nevertheless a cognition that makes life possible, precisely as sensory perception.

with their sensory perception - kant calls it reflection - animals fit into the constellation of their world and do from case to case what is expedient and sensible for them.

but precisely that is true of human beings as well, who certainly also make thinking, reason and understanding part of their sensory perception.

according to kant we experience the world not in the first place through reason, but through our sensory perception, and man's freedom is not to find the truth, but to fit into a world of functionality, autonomously, as a individual, but empathizing into meaningful perspectives. to this end we develop perspective designs of the world that are weighed up by sensory perception and thus become experience-judgements.

the world as design, life as design, directed by sensory perception of the concrete, that is a new philosophy.

when the first steam engine was invented by james watt in 1765, kant took up his first professional appointment at the university of königsberg. he was in the middle of the industrial revolution, thinking the first thoughts of a world that is not given by nature, but made.

3
19th century design philosophy was that "form follows function". this formulation comes from louis henry sullivan, an architect of the chicago school, who built the first building complexes without historical styles and used steel as a material in his structures in the same way as stone had been used before. the machine age is the application of newtonian celestial mechanics to technology and economics. thought was conducted in physical models. the success of power machines and motors gave wings to a mechanistic kind of thinking in which functionality shrinks to the notion of mere function. when sullivan used this formulation in 1896 he understood function in another

82

sense. the circling eagle or the open apple blossom, in short behaviour in nature was part of this concept. everything in nature is functional. but under the influence of the age, function was very quickly understood as a mechanistic linear connection between effort and purpose in the sense of mere exploitability.

the concept gained in strength, because it saw form and shape as a derivation, a relation, as the result of a methodological principle. for a long time the first buildings of modern architecture were labelled rationalist. but rationality is a characteristic, not a methodological principle. functionalist architecture on the other hand indicated a method. form was a result, a derivation from purpose and structure, not an outward appearance. modern building could be represented as a method, not as aesthetic appearance, as rationalist arrangement.

the new style was not only a different style replacing historical styles, it turned out to be a programme, a process.

in 1932 the italian architect alberto sartoris published a book on the architecture of his period. it was originally to be called *architettura* razionale. however, because of an intervention by le corbusier it was finally given the title *gli elementi dell'architettura funzionale.* here two different design principles are clear, design as a procedure and design as preparation of outward appearance. in the one case form is produced, as in craft work, from the material, the handling, the purpose, the use. in the other case an aesthetic entity, a style is introduced. these are two opposing positions like those of philosophy the one philosophy develops truth through a thought process free of contradictions, through a methodological approach, the other seeks out the truth as a given substance and introduces it.

rationalism in modern architecture is a style like gothic or baroque. it bears the stamp of an aesthetics of reduction and order in outward architectural appearance. it is classicism without cornices and comes from italy; it still continued to make its presence felt under mussolini because of the monumental gesture that is a characteristic of all classicism. rationalist architecture is undecorated neo-classicism with predominantly aesthetic qualities like symmetry or sequences.

functionalism on the other hand attempted to manage without stylistic principles and to solve architectural problems from the nature of the task and the means available.

even in the 19th century these opposing fronts were starting to emerge. viollet-le-duc took gothic as an example of architecture whose outward appearance emerged from the building method. at first this was difficult to understand, as gothic was seen as the style, as the symbolic form for all religious buildings. but viollet-le-duc showed that a cathedral looks as it does because the principles of building and structure made it essential. the pointed arch is not in the first place an aesthetic form, but the result of a vaulting principle, that of the ribbed vault.

gottfried semper represented the counter-position that was manifested in neo-classicism and the neo-renaissance. architecture is the manufacture of form. his major work was called *der stil* and identified architecture as based on the manufacture of forms of a spatial kind, forms of a structural kind and forms of a decorative kind. his model was roman architecture, which did not present itself as a building principle, but as a state-supporting manifestation, as an aesthetic gesture of power, as prestige.

certainly the notion of functionalism abbreviated the purpose-orientation of design to a more physical and mechanistic approach. building should bring more light, air and sun. in contrast with this the concept of "functionality" is broader. kant orientates it towards a kind of common sense. "functionality" stretches beyond "function". it also embraces psychological, social or economic dimensions, but not the principal task of style, which is to be a prestigious symbol.

functionalism is opposed to symbolic form and looking for a shape developed from the task in hand. this intention lent it a kind of provocative asceticism. functionalism turned a blind eye to all conditions that were not physical or physiological. the business of creating an expression of the times it left to expressionism and the business of creating an aesthetic presence to rationalism. it was also sceptical about the glorification of craft in so-called arts and crafts, which dedicated itself to the old methods with aesthetic enthusiasm. functionalism was the purpose-spirit of the machine age, of physical mechanics.

kant's concept of functionality was certainly directed at craft, not aesthetic arts and crafts, but the production culture that since the celtic iron age, particularly in combination with the working of wood, dominated material culture until the industrial revolution. kant was a saddler's son.

he lived all his life in a town the characteristic features of which were trade, but principally craft work. for a craftsman functionality is an all-embracing principle. it is true that the governing courts successfully demanded lack of functionality, decoration, ornament, adornment to express their higher claims and higher status, but correct craft work is distinguished by the highest possible level of correspondence between purpose and economy of effort. first and foremost the craft tool, but also farmers' equipment, tradesman's carts are the product of a culture of practical thought, in which a minimum of material and effort combine to produce an optimal performance with sovereign intelligence and love of the matter in hand. it is still a pleasure to hold a good craft item in one's hand. it radiates formal functionality, and this certainly also derives from the fact that the producer, the craftsman, followed the effects of his work by personal inspection. he was himself in the sphere in which his work was used, and in direct critical exchange with its users. this suggests that kant related functionality to common sense. it developed in production and in use by a community of manageable size.

industrial production exploded these direct spheres of experience. the up-and-coming railways led somewhere else, raw material came from somewhere else, and the goods were there to be sold anywhere and everywhere. common sense fled, and kant as well, as a republican, devoted himself to a world constitution and no longer only to people's rights in his own town and country.

craftsmen were replaced by engineers. design became a procedure in its own right as a specific profession. the designer was neither a maker nor a consumer. the criteria of his design work now came from abstract knowledge, from science, physics, mechanics above all, from chemistry, from physiology. appraisal was no longer the criterion of his work, not finding and intuiting but measuring and counting. he was not guided by *anschauung*, but by knowledge and calculation.

consequently functionalism as a design philosophy had to lead to a final reduction, dominated by calculation, guided by mathematical formulae and tables.

le corbusier proclaimed that his buildings were machines for living. he was aware that this was provocative. he consciously used sullivan's concept of function, to avoid the breadth of the concept "functionality" with its blurred boundaries. he wanted to reduce man to a biological being. he wanted to avoid subtlety and reduce sense questions to physiological behaviour. for him man's life was made up of eight hours of sleep, eight hours of work and eight hours of rest. man was neither a social nor a communicative being.

similarly the car was not a means of transport at that time but a technical end in itself, measured by speed and horsepower. it was not tailored to man and his needs but the converse, man was allowed to be involved in technological intoxication, in a technical artefact that took him somewhere, anywhere.

functionalism as a scientific interpretation and a mechanistic exposition of design was controversial from the beginning. architects like hugo häring, design theorists like kükelhaus missed the organic, formulation according to principles of life and the living. logical calculation without empathy was too tight for them, man as a biological being, living only on light, air and sun, too little.

admittedly functionalism cannot be reduced to a purely mechanistic interpretation, even if it likes to present itself as such as an ideology of the twenties, consciously and with a provocative stance. but without this rigorous approach it would not have been possible to develop a design practice that hannes meyer, for a time teacher and director at the bauhaus and close to the russian constructivists, described like this: "this building is not beautiful and not ugly. it is to be evaluated as a structural invention."

and indeed technology has given us a a world of products, from the bicycle to the umbrella, from the railway engine to the typewriter, from the paperclip to the posidrive screw, that aesthetically could neither be foreseen nor derived. technology relased a wealth of new aesthetics. hannes meyer also ran counter to formalism, which postulated an elementary aesthetic using circles, squares and triangles, which to a certain extent had to be imposed upon all industrial production as aesthetic transcendentals. he even came into conflict with the bauhaus, which saw itself as an artistic institution. he attempted to detach himself from all aesthetic obligations, in order to release the aesthetic of the thing itself. van doesburg or moholy-nagy stood by the primacy of form, which means the same thing as the hegemony of art. in their eyes the criterion for all design was pictures or the picture. art reigned supreme in the bauhaus.

they remained rationalists, and postulated an aesthetic existence above the concrete product. with persistent idealism they raised basic aesthetic forms to a superordinated principle and relegated the product itself to a mere case of application.

hannes meyer and the constructivists were certainly also prisoners of a style that today is being proclaimed a new fashion, but they sensed that without a provocatively formulated renunciation of any aesthetics they would not be able to achieve true outward appearance for the technical product.

here their thinking was scarcely different from that of a saddler's son from königsberg. form lies within the thing. but how can it be released?

4
ludwig wittgenstein began to train as an engineer. he worked on flying machines and aeroplane engines even before the wright brothers flew for the first time in 1908. his work on mathematics led him to philosophy. he was interested in the question of how thinking could be made more precise by a kind of mathematical logic. formalization of the steps taken in thinking was intended to bring more clarity and eradicate meaningless statements.

wittgenstein thought very highly of kant. They were both concerned with mathematics. kant kept to geometry, which is brought to life by pictures. wittgenstein remained attached to algebra, and raised the algorithm to the status of model for logical operations. thinking should follow a system of thought-steps, running like thought mechanics.

this made it necessary to have clear concepts, a language with precise expressions and statements. wittgenstein was convinced that "everything that can be thought at all can be thought clearly. everything that can be said, can be said clearly." at the end of the *tractatus* he said: "whereof one cannot speak, thereof one must be silent."

this last sentence was seen as a kind of philosophical fundamentalism. but for wittgenstein it was a technical-methodological problem. something can only be expressed clearly in language if it is precise. he could just as well have said: language-logical operations can only be carried out with clear concepts and statements. and so we forget everything that cannot be expressed clearly.

but precise language cannot capture everything in the world. what cannot be captured shows. and what shows cannot be said. with logic we cut out false statements and isolate everything that does not make sense. this includes everything that is beyond what can be said. it either has no meaning or it is wrong.

wittgenstein says that language disguises thought. the structure of thought is shown in logical-analytical operation. a logical operation of this kind is a kind of mathematical calculation of an algebraic nature. for this wittgenstein proposed an algebraic notation of his own with signs for logical steps. he thought he had created a complete system for finding truth, by means of which meaningless sentences can be separated from true ones, a kind of logical cosmology. he thought that this had solved the problems of philosophy.

later wittgenstein reversed his view. he then discovered that our concepts are not unambiguous, but have many dimensions. "what we teach is the different nature of concepts." it is not a language with exact concepts that is precise, but a language that can adapt to states of affairs. in language games language moves towards its objects and as it were opens up new dimensions of the concept. we do not come closer to things through logic as a system of exact statements, but through study, the description of language in use.

there is no longer a truth function. functionalism as a system of exact elemental statements, as a system of exact scientific operations, is superseded. a new criterion of truth appears: use.

listening and looking become an act of philosophy, and not a thinking operation within a complete system any more. wittgenstein is now saying to his pupils: "don't think, look!"

wittgenstein saw this transformation as painful. he now had to turn away from the attempt to establish a logical ideal language and agree that everyday language reveals the meaning of language, everyday use. it is in use that we see what language can capture and how it captures it.

this is a fundamental reversal, and wittgenstein was plagued by doubts about the world and about himself because of the collapse of a system-orientated view of the world. he thinks it is possible: "that mankind is running into a trap, that it is the end of mankind if it looks for a final systematic truth." there is nothing good or desirable about scientific cognition, he said. he was taking the error of the age upon himself.

what now emerges as a new philosophy is a revaluation of all values. its rule is: "we are taking words away from their metaphysical application and back to an everyday one." in metaphorical terms this means that the mind is not above, in the heights, there is nothing higher, the mind is in the thing.

logic collapses, we have to return to the things of everyday life.

today it is good to accept that there is an everyday culture alongside the great culture of the mind, and to turn to the lowly spheres of the common people, to more lowly work and trivial applications. everyday culture is a new catch-phrase that takes the upward surge of sociology into account and understands society not just as an élite, but also in its basics. people talk of a complete view of culture, taking ordinary things seriously as well as high art and sublime science.

things are different in the case of wittgenstein. he does not see a not-only-but-also, which would make a turn to the everyday a kind of alms-giving favour. he thinks the world out from the bottom, bases truth on use, everyday use.

here he is as bold as marx, who explains consciousness from the material culture of work, or the designer, who sees art as aesthetic mataphysics, and in designing does not turn to higher things, but to everyday use. the everyday is not a lower thing. "the most important aspects of things for us are concealed by their simplicty and everyday quality." we have to reveal them.

everyday language is not the materialization of the logical structure of language. spoken language is not application. and philosophical depth is not found with new words, it appears in revealing, describing and explaining the everyday. greatness is to be found in the ordinary.

in parallel with this, design is not application of a higher, artistic aesthetic to the everyday. concern with design at the point where it appears, in everyday use, opens up real aesthetic spaces. form becomes perceptible by approaching use, in following its operation, its variety, not in the esoteric gesticulation of art. the way an object is used, the way it is made, shows form and design. form cannot be imposed, not even, or precisely not, when it appears with the claims of art, just as little as language can be handled with logical systems.

"the more precisely we consider actual language, the stronger is the conflict between it and our requirement (for crystal clarity of logic). the conflict becomes intolerable. we have got on to slippery ice, where the conditions are ideal in a certain sense, but we also can't walk for that reason. back to rough ground!" super-ordination of logic with its super-concepts is in a vacuum.

super-aesthetics of pure form, which claims to make the spiritual manifest, whether it is the depths of the soul, the *zeitgeist* or the aesthetic as such, is in a similar vacuum. there is no aesthetic as such, even if it appears in mathematical considerations. the aesthetic lies in the thing.

wittgenstein is aware that he has left everything in ruins behind him. a pure arrangement of language was intended to appear, and everywhere there are fragments. he has to think again.

use reveals the correctness of things that fit together. use reveals fact. the constellation of what is correct is established by use.

with this a last purpose of the world disappears into the speculative distance. things are justified in the balance of assignment, in use itself, in proving themselves immanently, and in their own demonstration of the correct. there is no longer any heteronomy.

the prophet of rational clarity and calculation returns to the penance of describing use. just no more theory please. don't think, look! explanations must be swept away, to be replaced by description.

visual thinking, that kant understood as *anschauung* and aesthetic judgement, is applied by wittgenstein to the consideration of use. functionalism orientated towards science now leads to a description and not a reason. seeing how things behave, seeing how words are used, seeing how something is done. "it is not possible to guess how a word functions. one must look at its application and learn from it."

this is not intended to lead to behaviourism. man is not in direct contact with the world. we do not grasp the world as world, but in its copy as language. but we experience what language achieves by handling it. and philosophers should no longer talk about beings and their speech, but about table, chair and door. they should look at the language that is spoken.

in a similar way design is concerned with instruments, tools, artefacts, not with the world. but the way they are to look should no longer be determined by form, the aesthetic principle, but by use. form does not result from a code, however clear, not from art, but from application. just as the most precise logical calculation possible cannot approach the message of language, in the same way concern with pure form is an obstacle to understanding the appearance of an object or determining its shape.

without an attitude of this kind, without this kind of life-form, we are trapped in the cage of a self-created claim for purity, clarity, calculation. to approach language we should contrive language games, examine language models and set up algorithms of its modalities. it should be tested.

this kind of philosophy is an activity, is work. yes, it is an attitude, a point of view. wittgenstein uses the word "lebensform", "life-form" for it. language becomes accessible through language games from a particular life-form, from a particular way of handling words.

the affinity with design becomes increasingly clear. design is handling things before it can be knowledge. design renounces the aesthetic absolutism of art and looks for the aesthetic of use. not because the two things are different. just as the absolute calculation of systematic logic distorts the world, art as a message in principle distorts access to things. it adheres rigidly to its principles, repeats its methods, instead of finding close contact with facts and artefacts. the life-form of close contact with things and investigation of shape in models and experimental games is only possible by renouncing "higher things". what one gains is openness, an open sea. reality opens up.

otherwise it will not be possible to understand the language of technology in design, the language of minimal effort, the language of replacing force by intelligent structure, the language of networks of meaning, the language of the least extravagant structure, the language of structural variety and the language of handling.

in wittgenstein reflection about philosophy comes together with reflection about design. there are good reasons for this. wittgenstein was at home in the architectural debate of his period. he learned to understand architecture as work on oneself, similar to philosophy. thus he brought thinking and designing into line and used philosophy as an aid in design argument, and also design understood as an explanation-contribution to philosophy. there are no writings on the interconnection indicated here. wittgenstein worked with furniture, designed window furniture and door handles, but he never said anything about it. his philosophy itself is design philosophy, first one of functionalistic calculation, narrowing down a solution by calculation, then of phenomenal use.

functionality as kant understood it is organization directed at the senses.

functionalism is orientation towards knowledge and science.

use is the renunciation of everything that wants to explain, the thing itself expresses itself in its use.

striving for a final, definitive, fixable truth, for scientifically precise cognition is possibly the end of humanity. kant gave priority to aesthetic cognition of the rational conclusion. with wittgenstein and kant philosophy went off in a fundamentally different direction. this direction intersects with design. not only because wittgenstein did practical work in this field, but because design is concerned with the question: what can be manufactured, what should one manufacture?, and also moves towards philosophy's question: how should a world look that can shelter human beings, and how should the human being look who can prevent his world from calling him into question, even calling him physically into question? philosophy and design do not just have concepts in common. they follow a common path as well. they find out what should be from use.

philosophy and design are heading for the same point, philosophy in thinking, design in making. this point is that our world is in a condition of manufacturing itself. it is designed, it is made, we must see from use how good, how bad we are.

architecture and epistemology

it is thought that architecture and philosophy have few points of contact. but that is a superficial assessment. at the beginning of metaphysics is a creator who made the world like an architect, a masterbuilder. the world did not become, it was created, created to order-criteria for a diversity.
we do not know what god is. but we do know what an architect is, and so the architect has been elevated to the ranks of the divine. since that time we have interpreted the world as planned and ordered. we can no longer imagine an unplanned world, even if it is highly probable that it never was planned. the image of the creator making a plan and realizing his work to this plan, the image of the architect is so dominant that it not only distorts god but has also in our culture the measure by which we have to understand the world, that is, as planned.

everything that is the world has become so according to a plan, evolves according to this plan. this is built into our thinking like an etched pattern that cannot be polished out again.

a contrasting sentence to this could be: the world is everything that is the case. it is what evolved and is evolving according to the rules of probability and chance. it is a game, and its rules are the rules of the game. according to this the world would not be determined by timeless laws, but it would be constant variation, constant invention, constant design. certainly not without rules for the game, but without metaphysical determination.

but what would a philosophy do that could not devote itself to timeless laws? for the greeks, for plato and aristotle, and even for whitehead and russell the subject of philosophy was the general law, conformity with natural law, just as it was for the early wittgenstein.

greek philosophy would never have existed, and neither could western thought and european enlightenment, if it had not been for the image of the architect creating the world according to orders that we retrospectively perceive as laws. philosophy as the supreme discipline is only manifest if it is possible to investigate and reveal such laws, and metaphysics in particular is only possible if the orders of these laws can be investigated. but is this picture of the architect correct? do architects work like that? do they make plans in this way?

we want to know what the world is, where it comes from, where it is going to, where our place in it is and what determines and should determine our life. for this reason we use metaphysics when we want to look behind things, beyond what is given.

our critical understanding and analytical reason have however also come up with the question of what we can perceive at all, hope at all. the question about the meaning of the world is not so much a problem of the world as our own problem, in the form of a problem of cognition.

epistemology has replaced metaphysics for us today. anyone who wants to find out about the meaning of the world has to find out how we perceive, what we perceive.

one of the first to reverse the problem of philosophy was william of ockham, who addressed the question of whether general concepts are real, or products of thought. what is humanity? is it something superordinate that makes the individual human being possible, or is the human being there first, and then forms the sum of human beings, which we call humanity? and so is humanity only a word?

questioning of this kind caused the ancient view of the world to collapse. the concept of "modernism" emerges, the "via antiqua" is replaced by the "via moderna".

the ancients saw cognition as an objective problem, as a problem of how one gets to the bottom of the things of the world. ockham brings cognition into the subjective as a problem of how we arrive at concepts. ockham felt that he was forced into adam's position: he gave things their names. in the ancient world cognition was seen as participation in reality, as perception of the world, for ockham cognition was a creative act of word and concept formation. for him the world was evident as it is, but the concept of humanity was only possible when there were human beings. only after that were there concepts that sought to define what was human.

but for both plato and aristotle human beings were the result of a general idea "human being". the idea of the human being was there before human beings and stood above the individual human being, who was merely its embodiment. it was the architect of the world who created the human being, the real human being was only a copy. the old testament, which dates from the hellenistic period, is füll of this.

plato presupposed a realm of ideas of its own, in which the good, the true and the beautiful were at home. this realm of ideas was in his understanding beyond the world, and the concrete world was only a pale realization and materialization of this spiritual cosmos of primeval ideas. but the pure ideas were only imperfectly reproduced by materialization. matter, physical matter, only permits the pure idea to appear in inadequate form, everything physical is imperfect, simply because it is physical.

according to plato, cognition occurs because within ourselves we always remember the idea that lies behind a thing. via our soul, which comes from primeval times, we have access to eternal values and eternal truths.

three aspects may have led plato to this concept of cognition.

- in the traditon of pythagoras, plato was concerned with mathematics, particularly with the ideal fundamental bodies, which are still called "platonic bodies" after him today and are still the fundamental bodies of architectural construction. and here it is evident that in the world as it is, there is nowhere that we find the ideal sphere, the ideal cube or the ideal pyramid. mathematical bodies are superior to real bodies and pure only in their incorporeality.
- man perceives himself as a split being. his psyche and his mind are not infrequently in conflict with his body. man lives between permanence and emergent will, he lives between instinctive drives and control, and his physicality quite often gets in the way of his pure aims and intentions.
- plato took exception to the development of athens, his city-state. it was too emancipated and liberal for him, particularly under the influence of the sophists and their brand of critical and analytical thinking. a generation conflict became apparent into which socrates was also drawn when he was accused of corrupting youth.

plato's critique ran like this: we must do as the ancients did. the corruption of the world stems from the denial of eternal ideas, eternal values and eternal laws. the ancients had conquered the country, founded the new city states, created constitutions and laid down laws to control bondmen and slaves and for the best regulation of the business of the city. they had established science, and worked on developing the good, the true and the beautiful.

we are familiar with these arguments, that is to say that plato was an arch-conservative and approved of an authoritarian rather than a democratic polity. he appealed in his political writings for a council of the wise as the supreme political body. democratization and opening up the state, including slaves, went too far for him. it seemed to him that only a swarm of scholars had access to the realm of justice and truth that lay in the spatial and temporal beyond. and as far as beauty was concerned, the aesthetic roots of the well-proportioned and classical were also in a superordinate realm and were as binding as the laws of mathematics.

aristotle was a pupil at the academy that plato founded, a generation younger, and he did not wish to see political conditions bound to eternal laws, but determined by the principles of the common good. i.e., by that which is due here and now in the interests of all.

and aristotle was also not looking for truth in a far realm of ideal being, in the storehouse of the generally valid, as it were, he was looking for it in the world, in things themselves.

but he too got stuck with the idea of the plan, whereby plan meant something definitively valid, a complete prescription principle. things break down into their plan and their realization. it is as with the sculptor: he has an idea in his head, something he imagines, and has to hew it out of the stone as best he can. following this, according to aristotle things broke down into form and matter. form and matter were the basic concepts of his philosophy, with form expressing the spiritual principle and matter the physical.

man is form and matter, his consciousness is the shaping principle. as such it can also take on the forms of other things, stripped of their matter. by abstracting from experience, abstracting what has been perceived, i come to cognition and see the plan the things contain.

and so it is not longer the realm of ideas, but experience of the world as it is, that makes cognition possible, and the formal principle that constitutes things does not lie in the beyond but within them, as their forming principle. in saying this aristotle still assumes that matter only allows the spiritual principle to appear imperfectly, and for him matter is of value for nothing other than the isolation of a general idea.

according to this the individual human being, even socrates, indeed even aristotle himself, is only the random individuation of the idea of the human being. humanity, the idea of the human being, comes before the person.

early christianity was guided by this ancient philosophy, right down to the middle ages. but according to christian understanding it is no longer humanity, but the individual person who stands before god. the idea of the uniqueness of every human being in his character, appearance and behaviour developed from the jewish religion. and god is not an architect who drew up a world plan from which everything evolves and develops, god is a god of history who leads his people home from banishment, quarrels with them, punishes them and yet loves them. god is a god who speaks to everyone, comes to terms with them, even if a man like job despairs of him. in the jewish consciousness the world is in time, it has history, it develops. much of this went into the convictions of christianity. at first it did not break the cultural framework and cultural fetters of antiquity. the early fathers are accompanied by neoplatonism and even st. thomas aquinas uses the criteria of aristotle as a basis for his argument in his *summae*.

but the ancients never asked the question of how a plan emerges. well, how does a plan emerge?

the plan was seen as what was given, as a principle without time and evolution, as a prescribed structure according to which the way everything shall evolve is determined, as the generality that determines every individuation.

in the mean time we have learned from biology that there is no plan for the development of a species, whether we are talking about man or birds. blackbirds were not always as they are today, and will some time not be like they are today either. it could be that two species develop. it is the adaptations of individual blackbirds that determines their behaviour and stature and change them, often in tiny steps. cross-breeding within the species spreads subjective experiences and changes within the entire population and determines its development. and perhaps one day we shall need two words for the word blackbird because the species has split into two behavioural types that are also manifested in appearance. thus the species, the general, stands behind the individual. it is the individual that determines the species, not vice versa.

certainly the general exists in the sense of common features as characteristics of the group. but the general as something pre-planned and prescribed, as a determining guideline occurs neither in nature nor in the history of man.

this again does not mean that there is nothing in the world but single creatures, individuals. individuals join together in organizational forms, whether in families, working groups or states. for this reason marriage is no less real than the individuals that make it up. it is not just a name or a concept. but it is only real to the extent that it is realized by individuals.

marriage as an eternal institution, as a superordinate authority does not exist, however much even today the opposite is asserted in the spirit of current platonic values.

the world plan, that is the adjustment of indiviuals, whether singly or in groups, to the world. this plan can never be fixed in advance, even if it turns out to be meaningful in retrospect, and may even be in accordance with a law. every individual carries in his cells the development code in which adjustment experiences that the species has gathered are stored. the code is passed on in reproduction. it guarantees the behaviour patterns of the species as it has developed so far. but it does not say anything about how the individual will develop in concrete terms. he will do so within the framework of the pattern, but so freely that new kinds of behaviour can go into the hereditary code, regardless of how these new kinds of behaviour were triggered or came into being.

there is a plan for living creatures, for human beings and blackbirds. this is their behavioural code, their inherited knowledge, their genetic make-up. but this plan does not say anything about how they will behave in their lives in concrete terms, and also nothing about whether this plan will not be changed through the behaviour of the individual during his existence.

and so it is behaviour itself, adjustment to the environment and other subjects, work on harmonization with given surroundings, a search for a balance with the given conditions, the attempt to make optimal use of such interconnections that determine the plan, the plan of the species and the plan of the world.

modern science has suggested to us that there are constant laws of nature. this too is a reason to assume that there is a world plan after all, and also an architect for the laws of the world. but once the world as a whole was assumed to be mechanistic like a kind of device or machine, then the architect was increasingly replaced by an engineer.

now, ever since the earth has existed and turned around its axis the sun has risen every day. will it rise tomorrow? is that an absolute law? no. of course it will rise tomorrow. but it is possible to think that it will not. we have now acquired enough technical imagination to be able to conceive the end of the earth. but the probability that the sun will not rise again is so slight that it is equal to zero. and yet something extraordinary could happen. but what is the probability, when a raindrop falls precisely in the middle of a roof ridge, that it will run down to the left or the right? it is fifty fifty. the natural law of this process is that there is no natural law. any prognosis is wrong or random.

modern chaos theory, which is predominantly concerned with currents in liquids and gases - and what does not flow? - presents an alternative view of the world. yes and no, like this or like that, this is the law of the world.

and so how does a plan come into being?

how does the architect's cognition arise?

norman foster's office is unusual as far as its results are concerned. it is certainly unusual as far as the works as such are concerned, their quality, their appearance, their structural genius. but it is first of all unusual for the fact that the office has no style. each piece of work turns out so differently that one does not know what is going to come out of it next.

no less unusual is the fact, and this is perhaps the reason for the originality of every design, that the office has a design method that is perhaps the most highly developed of all.

whether one takes the renault building, the sainsbury centre or even the hong kong and shanghai bank there are always alternative designs for each commission. at least two designs are juxtaposed. for the sainsbury centre one has solid wall support and the other a grid support. for renault an umbrella concept with a support in the centre of the roof is set against a tent solution with four supports at the corners. the bank in hong kong was meant to be the best response to a false premise. the client wanted the building to grow in such a way that the old one could stay there until the new one was ready. this produced the building as bridge and the building growing in slices from back to front. there are numerous variants on this, which are not just stages of development, but counter-positions. fundamentally norman foster always makes double the development effort of other offices, because there are always at least two design approaches. the drop of water can run down to the right, it can also run down to the left.

le corbusier could not permit himself to do that, because the artist as architect only has one throw, even if this in fact develops. and mies van der rohe did not need to do it as he had a fixed style.

foster's alternative designs are not just stages, they are fully worked through as designs.

this working method makes it essential to develop the alternatives so perfectly that they can be compared in the final result. this does not necessarily mean that the designs run parallel in terms of time as well, they can develop one after the other, but their comparability must be assured by their being perfectly worked out.

comparability is ensured by representing the design in perspective drawings coming very close to reality, in technical drawings, particularly for details, and in models of model railway quality. reality is extorted.

in the case of all approaches to solutions it is not enough to present an idea, correctness must be proved. the structure must be developed, organization worked through and technical aspects of the building defined. only if the project is developed to the greatest possible extent can an informed decision be made one way or the other.

the first stage of the design is consideration of the nature of the task. this is followed by an analytical look at the surroundings. both local conditions and other model solutions are examined, if any such models have been produced. this analysis produces the first data for concepts. they are recorded in copious drawings.

the actual concept appears in the form of sketches. often these small sketches clearly anticipate the final version, at least as far as the appearance, the cultural dimension of the building is concerned.

norman foster is a magnificent draughtsman, but in a different manner from one's normal expectations of an architect. he has a clear inner idea, but a generous line that only intimates. the language of his drawings is that of giacometti. he looks for an inner reality and captures it. he is already able to walk through or around his buildings and is concerned with the moods they create.

other drawings capture technical or structural ideas. for norman foster the building is always built, a construction, and gains its character from structural characteristics. he is not just looking for a building, its organization, its face, but also a new structure appropriate to it.

but a concept is not yet a design. the seminar phase begins. the building is discussed, brought to a stage of rational clarity. seeing becomes making. the drawings become the size of drawing boards. ideas now become open to examination. but alternatives are still developing at the level of sketches, or are captured as the product of discussions.

the power of fact appears. only what will work now counts. this power is not hostile, not the rebelliousness of matter. on the contrary, fact inspires, it is the source of new possibilities, technical possibilities. this special form of architecture, that does not have its own style in either structural or aesthetic terms, comes into being by addressing what will work and will not work, what can be made and cannot be made, even if it has never been made before. this is the point at which the alternatives emerge. the counter-design appears alongside the design.

this produces architecture of which it could be said that mind is in the matter. addressing structure and technology is what produces the type, and they are not addressed because it is necessary, the discussion is sought. and so in this kind of architecture the organization-form of a building is not something that has to adapt to architectonic form, in the way that a monarch or an hotel can be accommodated in a palace. the organization-form is the result of discussion in which interconnecting systems can be just as much an invention as the investigation of new nodes.

it has never been possible to convince good cooks that there is anything other than the ingredients themselves, the material, that makes for very special cooking. one should forget recipes and sense how one can release the unique qualities, the character, the charm of what one has bought fresh at the market. a good cook merges with his food.

it is of the greatest possible importance to point this out if one is to form a picture of the way in which cognition comes about. architects and cooks, if they think anything of themselves at all, cannot allows themselves, like plato or aristotle, to see matter, material, as something secondary or even inferior. they do not have to be materialists if they are convinced of the fact that mind or spirit is in matter, that is the very thing that releases the material.

but what the material releases has to be brought out of it. the most time-consuming part of the design process consists of trials, experiments and studies, of countless cycles of examination and fresh starts using models and prototypes, with the assistance of one's own contribution and consultation with others to produce the distillate of the optimal solution.

the architect cannot be more clever than his material. but material does not say anything to an architect who is not clever. he remains without ideas. but what is a clever architect? one who can ask the right questions, not one who knows better.

and so is the cognition process in design a passive one? does the designer only participate in something that is already prescribed? by no means. designing is a creative process. from a certain point of view the material is passive as well. it only exists in certain forms of organization. and these are what has to be found. design is the manufacture of technical structural forms of organization and the translation of a programme into an organization.

material never appears as material in architecture. steel is in the form of half-finished goods, sheet, bar, profile, corrugated steel, and appears in the building as brace, header, tension or compression bar, as joint, as node, as screw, as rivet, as plate. steel is always shaped for a particular purpose. and concrete can appear as wall, as slab, as truss or pier, as bearer, and is reinforced according to its function. material is never aristotle's passive matter. he was using this concept on a high plane of art, not of industry, where the sculptor's stone did in fact represent something neutral. his interest in the organizational forms of material was minimal. he thought that plants and toads were made of the same substance. and indeed the importance of material is approaching zero in contemporary art as well.

designing is intellectual arrangement, clarification of links, definition of dependencies, creation of weightings, and requires a special ability in the head of the designer to be able to see and fix analogies, links and frames of reference.

architects are not scientists. they do not think in the categories of logic and do not draw conclusions, even when making judgements. they assess positions, classifications, frames of reference. they work algebraically rather than geometrically. they do not think in a linear fashion from conclusion to conclusion, but in networks, structures and interlinked systems. they evaluate in the spirit of optimizing the life form, the organization-form that releases a building.

a design is not finished when it is complete on this level. attention to real conditions, respect for the actual is so great that it is only the one-to-one model, the mock-up, that gives the security of definitive judgement. if the one-to-one model is good, the design is approved.

but the material challenge is not yet over, the dialogue between possibility and obligation not concluded. if a building is to be realized, a fresh start is made with another model, a prototype, at least for the parts covered by the concept of design and invention, the parts that have been newly conceived and found. and yet again the dialogue between conceptual and technical possibilities gets under way, and real examination provides an answer to whether a new version has successfully been derived from the field of what is technically possible. the prototype is tested and examined and subjected to every possible demands.it is clear that an architectural office like norman foster's works to methods that are also applied in the development of industrial products. in industry a distinction is made between
- task definition, programme
- concept
- design
- model examination, modification
- plan production
- development of prototypes

it is only after this that production can begin, and whilst every attempt is made to keep the expenditure of time, materials, work and costs to a minimum, as the complexity of the work increases there is a tendency to expand the basis and scope of the development. today development includes broad fields of research and the integration of many peripheral interdisciplinary areas. designing a car, a computer, a robot, but even an ingredient-friendly food processor is a broad collective effort that is inclined to exceed projected energy input and costs because there is

103

increasingly less hope of putting it back into plato's realm of ideas and waiting for inspiration precipitated by this memory.

important stimuli have come from modern technology for the dematerialization of material. we have already pointed to the fact that material appears only in organization-forms. this means that material, if it is harnessed in processes, and not just there, must be controllable.

an aircraft will not fly if it cannot be steered and a computer will not compute if it is not used on the basis of a program that has been installed, a programmed organization-form. a helicopter has over thirty fundamental forms of movement that can be controlled with the hands and feet. material too has a fourth dimension, it has a form of behaviour. this has produced extremely important philosophical concepts like those of software and hardware, even if they are pragmatic philosophical concepts.

software is the program for the organization of the machine, which is itself organized material. is plato ultimately catching up with us again? is there a spiritual element, an idea, without which technology cannot be activated?

wrong. the computer program that controls the machine's action field is part of the machine itself, emerges from it as a specific possibility. it is perhaps new in our awareness that programmes and control have a reality content, even if it is a soft one when set against the hard reality of material objects. we increasingly understand material as activated material, as organized material, and as such it is turned into machines of whatever kind. and machines are determined by programs and want to be controlled.

in the kind of architecture under discussion here there is no realm of architectural ideas. there is no aesthetic code. quite the opposite of current architectural theory.

this says that there are eternal architectural ideas, the column, the portal, the hall, the roof, the gallery, the balcony. the task lies in giving these eternal ideas up-to-date form in accordance with classical proportions. it claims that architecture is a dialogue standing above time about one and the same set of problems and is made recognizable by the quotation of earlier solutions.

philosophically speaking we have come back to plato, which also shows in the fact that the greek column and the greek pediment, the ancient triangulär pediment, the segment pediment and above all the broken pediment have become fashionable again.

matter, material is once more secondary to mind. it is used, whether it is concrete, steel or natural stone, as though it were dough, dough that can be shaped.

we have come back to the old function of the classical, which is to reinforce power by appealing to the eternal and the spiritual. but every personal individual life is a progress from experience to experience, from bitter insights to joyful insights, from narrow horizons to broad ones, from childlike landscapes to lifelike landscapes, from satisfaction to doubt, to revulsion and back to joy again. life is design and fate, we are thrown into it and yet have it in our own hands.

life is not classical.

classicism is an attribute of rule and serves to lend it authority as guardian of the eternally good, true and beautiful. classicism is the aesthetic expression of the conservative as a reinforcement of that which always was, in other words of might. nothing on earth wishes to stay as it was. only might uses all its resources to stay as it is. it resists the movement of the world, the life force. and this is why an attempt was made to establish a philosophy of continued existence, of the classical.

but this is not an exhaustive statement about contemporary architectural theory. hegel comes into it, we are walking the paths of dialectic as the form of cognition of world reason.

there is a great deal that is right about seeing modernism as the antithesis of historicism. it is also a way of coming to terms with the newly emerging world of machines, but also liberation from the aesthetic ballast of ornament, liberation from historical ingredients became the actual motivating force.

building in historical garments was once the highest form of cultural awareness, even if was also an alibi for the maximization of profit and the junk production associated with this. the antithesis to this was pure building.

and now the spirit of the age and hegel's world reason demand a synthesis of both. pink and turquoise iron girders leap out of natural stone cladding, bauhaus geometry is applied under the cornices of a new neo-classicism.

doubts occur about whether the system of dialectic as a way of deciphering world understanding and as a programme for the future can be valid if the most striking results are kitsch. what kind of a zeitgeist is it that is methodologically secure in philosophical terms, at least as a principle sanctioned by hegel and his successors, but which produces a mish-mash of inconsistencies and renunciation of thought?

even hegel's state seems not to have followed the cognition principle of dialectics, of world reason. at first this state was the principle of morality, by which the citizen had to be guided. then it was the principle of power and conquest. conquest of one's neighbour and conquest of the entire defenceless world.

then the state became the principle of economic reason, of the plan, of the command and welfare economy. and today it has degenerated to the inflated bureaucracy of tax collection and security checks. today the state is an institution that collects inordinate amounts of tax to maintain and secure its apparatus, two thirds of which is superfluous. could it not be that the zeitgeist, the spirit of the age, is a similar degeneration of the great weltgeist, the sprit of the world and its intellectual principle of progress and liberation?

what should we think of hegel's eternal laws if even plato's eternal ideas are leaving us in the lurch? what sort of a natural law is this, what sort of a principle of cognition that reduces the dynamic of world events and cultural progress to a logic that produces pure nonsense, neo-classicism à la bauhaus. in this case those architects are more consistent who precisely for the sake of preserving the status quo consider albert speer to be the most important architect of this century. speer kept to eternal architectural ideas. a portal was twenty times higher than a normal portal. the window was so large that it could only be opened mechanically, the foot of a pilaster, just the foot, was five times taller than a human being, and a storey was five or six times higher than usual. his dome could hold the dome of st. peter's a hundred times over and his triumphal arch made trajan's look like a garden gate.

it may be that it is still possible to establish a link with plato here. plato never said anything about size. and yet it is sheer inhumanity every time.

how can we arrive at architectural insights, how does cognition come about?

architects are not philosophers. architecture and philosophy hardly touch one another. apparently. architecture was a lowly field to which philosophy seldom descended.

this could change. if philosophy wants to concern itself further with the question of how cognition comes about, it must turn to making, the form of cognition that emerges from making.

the route to this was barred or made more difficult because philosophy seemed to be profiting from the denigration of matter, of material, of the body and embodiment.

western philosophy's hostility to the body or intellectual arrogance has finally led to the fact that the material in the form of organized technology has come over us like an alien force. we were not prepared for it, nor did we recognize this force, cope with it intellectually, or find ourselves in a position to control it. the disaster of the contemporary world is complete.

it would be good for philosophy to analyse and learn to understand cognitive processes at the point where cognition takes place. there are architectural offices that are like cognitive workshops. they crackle with intellectual discussion, problems arise that have to be tied up and brought under control, tamed by rational breaking of the spell. they invent and reject, formulate and forget, ordering systems are sketched, relationships established, and storms alternate with clear days. entire exploratory units search for an opening and a way out, a single idea sheds light. thesis is set against thesis. there is no search for eternal truth or the eternally beautiful. what is sought is correctness. and its authority is constantly brought in by means of trials, experiments with models, trial arrangements and dummies. trains of thought are followed as well as columns of figures and strings of data, the viewpoint moves from inner notions to calculation, and what one person divides up has to be co-ordinated by another. it is an adventure when insights and conditions come into contact in a concept and condense into a design, a form. views into the light alternate with night, there is breathing in and out, constraint and freedom, and nothing is more blissful than to have found the essence of something. applause would seem like a disturbance.

conclusion: cognition is work. work in the form of making. that means in the form of manufacturing models that can be compared. cognition is the naming of differences. which is more correct can be demonstrated from the alternative.

that is how architects work.
that is how nature works.

which method was used for planning the world? there has only been one philosopher who was also an architect, ludwig wittgenstein. after he had written his famous *tractatus logico-philosophicus* he built a house for his sister in vienna. this changed his philosophy. he developed a second philosophy. he had discovered the cognition that comes from making. truth, eternal truth, was replaced by what is correct, the rule of the game that arises from use.

wittgenstein, perhaps the most important philosopher of this century developed two philosophies. the first did not satisfy him. he had built a house.

use as philosophy

1 wittgenstein as an architect

wittgenstein built only one house, unless you count a small, conventional wooden house in norway in which he occasionally took refuge and that he used rather like a modest hide-hole.

but there are two reasons why this one house, haus wittgenstein in vienna, justifies talking about this aspect of his life. one reason is that it identifies wittgenstein as an architect; the other thing that concerns us is the unusual situation of a philosopher building a house. what does it mean when a philosopher builds a house, or an architect gets involved in philosophy?

the house as such is of considerable interest, entirely from the point of view that it was built by someone who influenced the thinking of our century like few other people.

an additional factor is that in the case of this philosopher as with few others we are witnesses to an inner, often painful movement, witnesses of a conflict that has found a whole range of interpretations right down to the present day. perhaps the house also reveals something about this conflict, which obviously occupied wittgenstein to such an extent that he never again thought or could think of building a house.

we can call it a unique house. it is unique, whichever way you look at it.

2 haus wittgenstein

haus wittgenstein was built from 1926 to 1928 as a house or perhaps better palace for margarethe stonborough, one of wittgenstein's sisters. she is known to us from a picture by gustav klimt in his gallery of beautiful women in vienna. she acquired the plot, a former nursery garden, in 1925 and commissioned architect erich engelmann, a friend of wittgenstein's and the family, to provide a design. wittgenstein was at the time a primary-school teacher in a village in lower austria, and was at first involved simply in discussion about the designs. wittgenstein gave up his post as a primaryschool teacher, and as he was undergoing a psychological crisis, engelmann involved him fully in the architectural project, particularly as he felt that wittgenstein understood his sister gretl's intentions better than he did.

engelmann knew adolf loos, one of the fathers of modern architecture. his villa steiner, dating from 1911, had provided an important prototype. wittgenstein himself spent a lot of time with loos, but found him a little too vain.

engelmann says himself of their work together that although the ground plans were already complete when wittgenstein became involved, he certainly considered him to be the architect, so great was his influence. wittgenstein was 37 years old at the time.

wittgenstein had completed his *tractatus* years before, it appeared in 1921. the book was immediately recognized as one of the most important of the century, even though or perhaps because it could only be understood by a very few people. but if bertrand russell or moritz schlick, the great mind of the wiener kreis were of this opinion, that should be enough. it is still highly esteemed today, even though - and wittgenstein would agree with this - it is a fossil.

after working on the house at 19 kundmanngasse, wittgenstein went back to england and began to conceive his philosophy mark II. thus haus wittgenstein is a piece of work that falls between the two philosophies, the tractatus and the *philosophische untersuchungen*, a period in which wittgenstein had temporarily suspended his work on philosophy. the house is an act in no-man's-land. it stands between the fronts of wittgenstein's first and second philosophies; they were torn apart from each other in torment.

margarethe stonborough took over from her parents the idea of an upper-middle class residence as a meeting place in which members of society and the artists of the metropolis could meet in an open social climate responsive to new ideas. almost the whole of the ground floor is given over to this purpose, with a room for intimate concerts, a dining room, two terraces, a hall and a room for salons. otherwise there was only a living room and a bedroom on the ground floor, probably for the lady of the house herself.

the first floor contains a flat with two bedrooms, a secretary's office and servants' rooms. the third floor was for children and the staff associated with them.

the basic shape of the ground plan is a T. the central section is the three-storey main building, the transverse section has two storeys. but the building does not have a simple, symmetrical form. it gives the impression of being various clear geometrical cubes pushed inside each other. there is no central axis. one is reminded of the design principles of de stijl and suprematism, especially as developed by malevich. it cannot be excluded that this was a contributory factor to wittgenstein's later toying with the idea of settling in russia.

in each of the corners of the T, where the main section meets the transverse section on the ground floor, are slightly raised terraces that create a relationship with the garden around the house and were particularly suitable for occasional social meetings. here the house has large french windows, making it very light, even though the room in the middle is completely closed, because of the concerts, and even has steel doors. on the ground floor the house is a house for events, and this explains the T-shape. the two-storey transverse section, the transverse bar of the T, is on the street side and acts as a screen. any meeting in the hall, the main room and the two adjacent terraces cannot be seen.

otherwise the rooms in the house are conventional, rooms with windows like anywhere else. the height is different on all floors. the ground floor, with concert hall, entrance hall and main room is 3.8 m, the living floor 3.0 m and the children's floor 2.8 m. correspondingly there are three different window heights. the large windows, mostly coming right down to the floor, are on the ground floor. the windows in the middle floor, even though some of them come down to floor level as well, are somewhat lower. the top floor has windows appropriate to the low rooms, most of them of normal design as windows with ledges.

and so one characteristic of the house is window articulation featuring high windows downstairs and low ones upstairs, with a high cornice above them. almost all the windows are the same width and have the same distribution of bars, producing four broad areas of glass. the window is only divided vertically, like windows in france it has only two cornice bars as a horizontal barrier.

the walls are in brick, and the ceilings, joists and bearers are in concrete. outside the house was light grey, inside white throughout. the windows were light grey.

as a whole the house makes a radical impression, purist in its reductiveness. clear, autonomous sections of the building with a flat roof are fitted together to produce a cubic form that makes an impression that is absolute but not totalitarian. nothing in it can be changed. but the windows are delicate. the whole thing is a fortress of grace, a manifestation of reduction. something so spare demands the highest possible precision in detail. wittgenstein, who originally wanted to become a mechanical engineer, devoted himself meticulously to the window and door furnishings, almost reducing the craftsmen to despair. there is no timber in this house. windows and doors are specially designed steel structures. here too wittgenstein is a pioneer, and his door handle has become the door latch per se in the last twenty years. this bent cylindrical tube can now be seen all over the world. does the house not even have a certain brutalist logic? a certain rebellious claim to clarity, purity, renunciation?

anyone who knows the *tractatus* immediately sees a will to ultimate reduction. there it says: anything that can be said can be said clearly. the world consists of facts. elementary sentences are copies of these facts. if we purify these sentences by the use of precise logic we have solved the problems of philosophy. *tractatus* and building exude the same rigour. there a distilled form of thought, here the fabrication of pure form, totality of aesthetics.

from today's point of view the house has features of architectural rationalism, as it emerged from futurism. it does not have the freedom, wittgenstein would later say the wildness, of le corbusier's buildings. it is disciplined in the same way as the sentences of the *tractatus*, with their decimal classification. it makes a very ordered impression, but it is never classical in the sense of prescribed aesthetic form. there are no artistic prescriptions, no formal code. the house does not repeat itself, it is free in a different way at every point and from every side. and yet it does exert a certain degree of constraint. the sections of the building seem unalterable. it is significant that wittgenstein would not even allow curtains.

we have to take a look back in time. the twentieth century had just started to discover itself.

this happened in vienna in the struggle against jugendstil. karl kraus campaigned against elegant writers like hugo von hofmannsthal and thomas mann. georg trakl wrote poetry opposed to edification of the soul. oskar kokoschka distanced himself expressionistically from the sweetness and fashionableness of

haus wittgenstein in vienna was built by ludwig wittgenstein for his sister margarethe stonborough from 1926 to 1928. the photograph shows the house from the garden side. the building would have been pulled down in the seventies if a word had not been put in by certain people who were at the time aware of wittgenstein's importance, pointing out the links between wittgenstein's philosophy and his views on architecture and design.

painters like gustav klimt. and adolf loos announced that ornament - and jugendstil was nothing but ornament - was crime. and he meant that quite literally. he considered that a society that spent its time bedecked in wealth and beauty, in an aesthetic world, and at the same time exploited the have-nots, was repugnant. at that time an individual country, indeed an individual town, looked as the world looks today, where the wealthy industrialized countries have become richer and more beautiful and the poorer countries poorer and more wretched.

it could still be said today: the culture of the colour supplement, of the drawing room, the solemn use of material is a crime.

wittgenstein knew the agents of this reversal personally, and himself saw the period as an earthquake. this earthquake also derived from his own person, his self-despair, his purism, his personal ethic.

wittgenstein was born in 1889. he studied engineering in berlin and manchester, and while still a student developed an aircraft engine with reactor jets on the propellor tips. questions of calculation brought him into contact with mathematics. he read frege's books on arithmetic and *principia mathematica* by russell and whitehead, which had just appeared, and at the time the outstanding works of mathematical logic. wittgenstein went to cambridge and attended lectures by russell, who even moved him to give up aeronautics and turn to philosophy. he was rapidly accepted into the society of the cambridge greats. he met russell, whitehead, moore, lord keynes, eccles. but after two years he withdrew to norway, to work alone on logic. there he built a little house for himself by a lonely fjord in the forest. it was 1914, the year of the war. after his father's death he inherited a large fortune. he gave it back to the family. he wanted to remain poor. he gave money to some literati, intellectuals and artists recommended to him by ludwig ficker, the editor of the magazine *brenner*. these also included adolf loos.

he went through crisis after crisis. he said of a book like tolstoy's short *explanation of the gospel* that it had saved his life. ten years earlier he had said the same of william james, who had awakened his interest in religion. he read kierkegaard. his life became a landscape füll of ethic appeals to himself.

during the war he was an austrian soldier on the eastern and italian fronts, where he was taken prisoner. he completed the manuscript of his *tractatus logico-philosophicus* while on leave in 1918. the book was originally intended to be called the *sentence*, the new title was suggested by moore. moore was the most important philosophical personality in cambridge. russell wrote a foreword, even though he maintained that he could not understand the whole work.

wittgenstein thought briefly of entering a monastery, then became a primaryschool teacher, a profession of self-prescribed moderation. but he was not suited to it.

this brings us to the time at which wittgenstein built the house for his sister.

it is obvious that he did not do this because he wanted to become an architect. haus wittgenstein shows that wittgenstein could have made a contribution to the new ideas about building, but that is not what it was about.

he later said: "work on philosophy is - perhaps like work in architecture actually more like work on oneself. on one's own view of things. on the way one sees things (and what one demands of them)."

later wittgenstein finds that the house was the product of "decidedly refined hearing, good manners and the expression of great understanding". he interprets manners as style, and by understanding he meant openness to the culture of the period. the somewhat cryptic sentence is probably saying that he had paid a lot of attention to adolf loos and his current environment of new building. but wittgenstein is more decisive and remorseless than loos. loos is looking for plainness, but often wallows in materials that he drags in from great distances regardless of expense. what is clear is that wittgenstein considers loos to be one of the few people who influenced his life, along with kraus, boltzmann, schopenhauer, frege and russell.

another of wittgenstein's sisters condescendingly called the house "petrified logic", "a house for gods", even though she admitted that margarethe stonborough flourished there and that it was luminous with her personality.

later wittgenstein was to call logic an ideal language in a vacuum, and recommended that philosophy should go back to being conducted in everyday language. but at that time logic was everything for him.

there is unquestionably a family resemblance beyween the tractatus and the "house for gods".

this brings us to the question of the relationship of this piece of work by wittgenstein to his philosophy and the effect of philosophy on the architecture. we are not interested in the house at 19 kundmanngasse so much as an architectural-historical monument as an unusual interrelationship between thinking and doing.

there were examples of semiotic analysis of the building to prove direct derivation of the building from the *tractatus*, or perhaps the philosophy that was just beginning.

the *tractatus* contains a great deal about structure, form and formal sequence in the context of forming an elementary sentence. for example, it says: "(5.232) the internal relation that orders a sequence is equivalent to the operation by which one term emerges from another." is this mathematical statement also to be understood as an architectural reference?

wittgenstein expresses himself very cautiously about this. in his own words there is "perhaps" a relationship between philosophy and architecture. he is not sure. to this extent we shall not attempt here to try to find the philosophical theses in architecture as well, to understand architecture to a certain extent as a copy of philosophy, however much related things are to be perceived as appearance, as habitus.

nevertheless there is an amazing interrelationship between wittgenstein's philosophy and his building. to this end it will be necessary to give an interpretation of wittgenstein's two philosophies, though this should be prefaced with the remark that if even bertrand russell said that he did not fully understand wittgenstein, one does not which to claim too much certainty for oneself.

it will be impossible to avoid going into the philosophy in rather more detail. i shall do this partly in my own words, as i see it myself.

3 we in the world

does language copy the world? this is wittgenstein's original problem. at first he thought that language was a copy of the world. is it?

wittgenstein sees logical thought as a copy of causality in the world process and copies each from the other. thus anyone who thinks correctly can make true statements about the world. it is only a matter of thinking cleanly, and we have correct insights into the world. cleaning up thinking methods by the use of logical calculation means solving the problems of philosophy and that means that we understand the world.

this is how wittgenstein thinks in his first philosophy. a few critical reflections of a quite general nature about this.

the pictures that i form for myself of the world are private, entirely my own and confidential. i see a tree. the image of this tree reaches my memory as soon as i look at it more attentively, more purposefully. i see a number of trees during the day but do not perceive them. but as soon as i look at a tree with interest it is so well established in my memory, so stamped there that i can remember it. this memory is private, and belongs to me alone. noone looks into me to whom i do not open the window. man is firmly integrated into the world in various ways.

anyone familiar with life in the desert has the clear experiences that after two days without water a man is dead. water in the earth and water in the body are synchronized. it is the same with air. if i stopped breathing in oxygen from the air i should be dead in minutes. i am firmly linked to the world by oxygen. it is similar with food. it is possible to live longer without food, but the life of animals in particular is to a large extent exclusively concerned with maintaining the metabolism that binds them and us to the world and with which we take the world into ourselves. in many ways our relationship with the world is similar to a fixed transmission. it is additionally very personal. every bird breathes for its own lungs, eats its own food, with the exception of bringing up its young, and drinks water for itself alone.

here man has certainly been successful in intervening in nature. food can be collected for as long as it will keep. i can then share it with someone else, the shell of individuality is broken open, nourishment is shared with colleagues. the connection with the world, which is originally an individual one, determined by a linear relationship between me and the outside world, is given one more direction, one more dimension, that takes us to our fellow men. social behaviour is added to world behaviour.

this develops into a new form of existence through the possibility of storing, husbanding food on a larger scale by preserving it. fire brought methods of sterilization by boiling, frying, smoking. now so much food can be stored that the original individual world relationship became an emphatically social behavioural organization. people started to stay in the same place, did not have to move around looking for food all the time like animals, people began to share out work, one cooked and preserved, the other brought up the children, a third made pots, a fourth tools for hunting, a fifth dedicated himself to physical and psychological medicine.

something similar happened to our perception of the world, our seen and stored pictures. we began to share ourselves out into perceptions by preserving pictures in words and passing them on through language.

we created a now copy, the word, from the copy of a tree in our memory.

this copy was not at all similar to a tree, just as jam is not similar to an apple. in german the copy of the copy is the word "baum", in french it is called "arbre", in english "tree". the picture was translated into sound signs. if there had always been something in nature like paper and something like ink perhaps we would have got into the habit of making a drawing, a pictogram as the copy of a copy. drawing and writing would then have come before speaking. but we used our hearing and the sound signs as a medium for making our copies of copies, and thus making them communicable to other people.

if one says that culture has an angle of 90 degrees, this indicates the fact that i convert my outer relationship with the world into a social relationship with my fellow man, by cooking and by speaking.

the world contains things and processes. i perceive them visually in the main and retain them in my memory as pictures. the copy of these pictures is no longer visual, but an acoustic sign of a random nature that is fixed in a convention and that has to be learned. in learning i attach a meaning to a group of sounds like t-r-e-e. a language that I have not learned is absolutely incomprehensible to me. i can learn it, if necessary without a teacher, if i make a relationship between the sound signs and the objects and processes in the world. i point to a tree, say the word tree and fill the sound sign with its meaning, its sense.

so language is not a copy of the world, but a copy of the pictures that copy the world. it is an acoustic copy of the visual pictures. it refers to the world only indirectly. only when learning the language do i relate to the actual tree, after that i can talk about trees without seeing any.

our food has made itself independent of nature. methods of conservation using boiling, frying, smoking, and later salting and sugaring, have created a second nature. we now know products that do not exist in the world as world. soup, roast meat, dessert, menus, spicing, jam, cheese, butter and dripping do not occur in nature. the starting point is natural produce, but it is transformed into culture-products by technical change.

language is detached from nature in a similar way. it is no longer a medium for absorbing the world, but for processing and passing on what has been absorbed.

this processing of pictures we call thinking. thinking means comparing pictures and establishing differences. the form of this comparison is again a picture, but the picture of a relationship. this is copied in language as a sentence.

wittgenstein used the original copy theory to demonstrate that language and thus pictures of the world had a logical structure. this would make philosophy the purification of language from anything that does not fit in with the logical structure of pictures. if language were purged of nonsensical expressions we should understand the world. nonsensical expressions come into being when words no longer agree with the facts of the case that they copy, and when words are linked with false words in sentences. linking forms are defined in logic.

and so if the logical form of all sentences is found, one would grasp the structure of all true sentences. this was the essence of wittgenstein's first philosophy. and wittgenstein was involved in the attempt to fix logically meaningful links by using mathematical signs, and thus making the discovery of truth into a process of calculation.

this was followed, as we know, by a long period of silence. critical examinations followed, by ramsey and sraffa, for example, and then the insight that there is no such thing as identity in the world, just as little as there is a system of weeks or the decimal system. the world counts neither days nor their quantities. we could also understand the world in a different system of measures or in other sequences of numbers.

counting is a help to comparison, and thus to thought, it also finds its home in thinking. it is part of the language of thought, is a culture form. it is only possible to copy the world using the object-language. in the language of thought communication, the exchange between two memories, the structure is normative, set, found. just as the cook's menu is made, manufactured in the kitchen. nature does not provide the kitchen with recipes, only with raw materials.

wittgenstein noted that mathematics is an invention, not a discovery. language is a tool, not an illustration. and tools are not illustrations of natural mechanisms. there are no metre rules, no books, no clocks, no hammers in nature. these are inventions.

in his second philosophy wittgenstein sees language as a tool and philosophizing as work. he rejects tricks of a logical nature and sticks to spoken language, everyday language, and describes what happens in it. he does not reduce it to calculation.

he no longer measures the meaning of the word as a copy of the world by the world, but in the use of language, its effectiveness. the point remains that language means learning, identifying sound signs with the things of the world. meaning is borrowed from reality, but ultimately emerges from use, the way the word is used in its technical, instrumental quality.

there is such a thing as a tree, but there is also a public house called "the tree", there is a family tree and a family of trees, the tree of knowledge, the tree in the avenue and the world-tree.

wittgenstein now sees language as an instrument of a world that is not pre-existent but made, a world of thoughts, and he sees speaking as a technique. it is permissible to take these concepts literally.

man does not only take food from the world as the material for his metabolism, he does not just take over pictures and perceptions, he also takes over products and objects from the world in his development.

once this was wood for the fire, stones as tools, fur for clothes. here too there is a direct relationship with the world at first, that gradually turns into the invention of man's own products like the wheel, which of course does not occur in nature, just like vertical walls. then man steps into a world of his own: he builds houses, machines, he invents industrial production and arrives at a diversity of products approaching nature's wealth of species. he lives in a designed and made world as a species and as an individual. he develops forms of working, dwelling and living. and this is not done using an objective model, according to what is determined by being, but according to his own concepts and abilities.

until our day the world has been understood as "being" in which we are embedded, no matter whether we experience this world empirically or transcendentally. the fact that in the mean time we have come to live in our own world of science and technology, of our own thinking and making is according to wittgenstein wrested with difficulty from the philosophical tradition. but wittgenstein refers to no philosophers and no philosophy before him. he knows that cognition occurs in language, and he searches language, first language as copies of the world, then language as an exchange of memories and consciousness, as a thought language of a world given and made only to and for man. we live in our own structure of economy, of industrial production, new forms of organization, new rules of behaviour and new forms of communication.

wittgenstein sees language as made, according to which rules we use in various language games. and the criterion for its justification is use, what language is good for. philosophizing means showing that we live in languages, and means showing how we use languages.

4 use

use, the last criterion of language?

a concept hitherto unknown to philosophy suddenly rises to the highest rank. we no longer talk of the transcendental, of the ding an sich, of experience, of trial and error, of truth. we talk of use, of use not as a testing category, as a sieve, that separates the true from the false, but of active use that makes what is correct. it is in use that a word arrives at its meaning, in use that language creates new ways of seeing. use is like a game, a language game. rules are set, the rules of the game, and new reality begins to develop immediately. but game rules are not right or wrong, they prove themselves in use and are right or wrong according to their value in use. language becomes action, becomes making, and makes up a form of life. language games, today we would perhaps say language culture, develop in action, in manufacturing, in handling things.

anyone who says sunday, the day of the sun, not of work, introduces a new fact into the world, just like the person who coined the expression social darwinism. the first person to say metre created a new perspective from which to see things. the decimal system gave us a different view of the world from the duodecimal system. the advantage of the duodecimal system lies in use, in its greater divisibility.

the concept of use is not just highly prosaic, it comes from a quite different direction from plato's "idea" or aristotle's "entelechy". it does not come from the fields of the mind, not from the depths of being. this word is the culmination of wittgenstein's notion that truth lies in the everyday and ordinary.

there is no question about the fact that the concept comes from the views of adolf loos and the foundation of functionalist architecture, and further back it comes from william morris and john ruskin, the british arts and crafts movement that rediscovered craft culture after the bombast of baroque and classicism, that had produced the medieval city, cathedrals and concrete thinking. "use" as a concept also goes back to the positivism of mach and boltzmann and the all-dominating significance of the experiment in modern science. but for wittgenstein use is more than practical examination, the concept approaches that of behaviour. thus it also refers to american pragmatism, although you will not get close to wittgenstein with the notion that the world puts its stamp on men.

and finally it is no surprise that the concept of "use" acquires the highest philosophical honour when you have it before your eyes that wittgenstein handled machines and apparatus throughout his life and there are numerous anecdotes about all the things that he repaired and got working again. like loos' architecture, wittgenstein's philosophy refers to the reality of modern technology.

here a reservation should be made. it is true that wittgenstein works on the basis that "the whole of culture is part of a language game". he took the example of music in vienna to explain that it is musical use that produces music. but for him this use is not just creative design, but the "transmitted background". language games operate on the basis of what is given, what is generally customary.

wittgenstein perceives the customary as the unknown. it is unknown and unthought about because we customarily do it. and so the work of the philosopher is to dig out the known and illuminate the everyday. then the achievement of philosophy is not to penetrate the depths, but to discover the surface, to describe that in the use of language which is apparent, but not seen, only used. there are philosophers of depth. wittgenstein is not one of them.

thus for wittgenstein the concept of "use" includes not just making, but also what is made, learned, passed on. we make ourselves understood on the basis of what has been handed down, reach judgements about what is true and false, acquire convictions for communal action. but these things that have been handed down are not a norm, we have to find that. and to this end we invent our language games, so that the use of language can show what is already given, but not seen or shown.

this means that philosophy is work. work at one's own view. acquiring one's own view through work.

work on the way in which things are to be seen. and work on what one asks of things, what they yield.

this work is philosophy. and:

perhaps work in architecture not with architecture, not as architecture but in architecture is the same thing.

and that is how one has to see things, what they yield.

a view of things is developed for one's self and from one's self.

did wittgenstein finally see philosophy as work because he had made the discovery as an architect that there is no architecture except the architecture one builds?

there is no question about the fact that here thinking and making, philosophy and architecture are being related to each other in a most unusual way, by defining even philosophizing as work, as an activity, like building.

philosophy is not a system of values, not a possession, it is something that is done. philosophy is no longer a doctrine, it is manufactured.

a scholar with whom wittgenstein was friendly, the economist lord keynes, was concerned at the same time with the role of money and established an economic theory that has since become central. it too says that money is not a value, it has no substance, it is work. is is itself something that can be exchanged for work and is only used sensibly if it works. it is not a possession, but an application.

a parallel of this kind can be coincidence. but it is no coincidence that lord keynes sees money and traffic in money as something more like an invention than a natural law. and that its value lies in its use.

money, like language is a means of exchange. we can see money as a material language game in the sense of wittgenstein. if we do that we must also say of money that its value lies not in something that it covers, but in its use.

it is somewhat heretical to talk of money in the same breath as wittgenstein's philosophy when he lived throughout his life in self-imposed modest circumstances. but we are only taking it as a model. and thus it may become clear that anyone who sees money as worth something and saves it in a stocking does not know what money is and is in danger losing it. money is dealing with things, in both senses of the word. dealing means being active, making something, and it also means dealing in the sense of selling something in the market place. only people who handle money acquire its value, and perhaps increase it.

here use has the active sense meant by wittgenstein when he sees langauge as action. in his eyes it is action in the context of one's own life form, with one's own customs.

wittgenstein's friend keynes was concerned almost exclusively with money, and recommended an almost contradictory custom, that of deficit spending. earning money can consist of spending it and saving money can mean losing it. but this too is not a general statement, and refers much more to the situation, the context, the case. every language game has its own rules.

it is not far from money to mathematics. what wittgenstein says about mathematics may again make clear how far away wittgenstein is from that theory of being that works on the premise that we are natural beings, live in "being" and not in a new world, developed by man, of cultural, technical and social artefacts. for wittgenstein mathematics too is not discovery, but invention. it is a language game with numbers connected to operations by the rules of the game. it is not based in "being", that is something there to be discovered like a strange part of the world, it is a constructive intervention. it is just as unreal as the meridians on the globe. these are nowhere to be found. it also does not matter whether the earth is divided into 360 degrees or 400 or 16 or 10. the division is just a form of parcelling, in order to be able to speak about the earth in a more precise, denser form. it is like a set of shelves that allows us to store more objects in a more manageable and tidy way.

now how does wittgenstein himself see the difference between the philosophy of the *tractatus* and the philosophy of the *philosophische untersuchungen*? one sign of his incorruptibility is the fact that one can rely on judgements that affect him. the judgement is unambiguous. here is a series of quotations:

in the *tractatus* he was a logician who "finally showed mankind what a correct sentence looks like", it was as if "(he) was speaking within the logic of an ideal language. as though our logic were a logic intended for a vacuum, as it were." but logic does not stand outside language and also does not confront it in the way that science confronts a natural phenomenon. in the best case it is a structure, a "constructed ideal language". but this too would be misleading, "as that sounds as though (the ideal language) might be better, more perfect than everyday language."

he said that at that time he had constructed a language for a vacuum, created a new kind of idealism and behaved as though there were a more perfect sentence than those spoken in our everyday language.

he now no longer wishes to explain what happens in language, does not want to play the know-all, but to describe, in fact he goes as far as to say "don't think - look!"

he had "got on to a false trail where it seems as though we have to describe the ultimate refinements that we do not have the means to describe." in doing this we had to "see that we have to remain with the things of everyday life." "we take words back from their metaphysical to their everyday application." for wittgenstein logic, as he says, has broken up.

"the aspects of things that are important for us are hidden by their simplicity and everyday quality."

"every sign seems dead on its own. what gives it life? it lives in use." through application in life, in a certain form and agreement with life, in a life form, that is where a sign acquires its meanings.

"it is impermissible to set up a theory. we must get rid of all explanation and replace it with description alone." it is no longer wittgenstein's aim to achieve precision and crystal clarity of statement. "we must look over the sentence," as has been said, "don't think, but look!"

in a kind of atomism, wittgenstein once attempted to find elementary sentences that could be broken down no further, sentences corresponding to logical operations and equations. when these are found the problems of philosophy are solved. atomism was joined by a claim to absoluteness. now this rationalism is suspect to wittgenstein. a new philosophy pursues language as a whole, wants to acquire an overview, not compelling statements, and understands it as an activity, not as a system.
wittgenstein speaks of serious errors that he has made. he extends this into a general statement: it is "not nonsensical to believe that the scientific and technical age is the beginning of the end of mankind; that the idea of great progress is a delusion, and so is that of a final perception of truth; that there is nothing good or desirable about scientific cognition and that mankind is running into a trap in striving for it."
this is the judgement of a man who himself wanted to make thinking more precise, who was considered the strictest proponent of logical analysis, who wanted either rational clarity or nothing.

5 school of making

it is unusual for a philosopher to develop two different philosophies in his lifetime. it is even more unusual for him to admit his own mistakes. this honesty is appropriate to the fact that for wittgenstein philosophy means an ethic. it was - like architecture - work on oneself. this is the only way of explaining the great span encompassed by someone who wanted to force truth through the press of mathematical logic, of science as science, to someone who suspected that scientific thought could be the trap in which humanity would find its end. thus he judges as a man of rational thought for whom the "pneumatic", intellectual thought, was a horror.
does haus wittgenstein have a place in this span? wittgenstein himself links architecture and philosophy like no-one else. "work on philosophy is - like perhaps work on architecture - actually more like work on oneself. on one's own view. on the way in which one sees things (and what one demands of them)."
according to this wittgenstein - perhaps - learned from his building how to see things and what he could demand of them. it was work on himself.

to all appearances haus wittgenstein is logic turned to stone. if this were so it should be ascribed to the first philosophy, that of the *tractatus*. but does it also relate to the second philosophy? and what is the key word in the second philosphy? it is "use". where does this concept come from? it had previously never cropped up in philosophy, certainly not as a central concept. and can use be discerned in a building, as one doubtless can discern the effects of the strict and rigid calculations of logic?

as the only thing other than philosophy that wittgenstein mentions as something that has taught him a particular view of things and what they should achieve is architecture, then it is easy to conclude that it was work on this building that taught him the key concept for this second philosophy, that of use, made him experience it, impressed it upon him and made him absorb it. the building whose appearance is the embodiment of the *tractatus* would at the same time according to this have been the school for his second philosophy, and his second philosophy would be one of design, of a life-form, it would be teaching that it is through use as an individual action and through use as a criterion that one comes closer to oneself and to things. A great saying of a new, a great philosophy would be recognizable in its place of origin, 19 kundmanngasse, vienna. it is not compulsory to see things this way, but it is permissible. for wittgenstein himself says that it was architecture as well as philosophy that taught him how to look at things.

a second concept is just as new and unusual as a constituent element of a new philosophy, that of the language game. speaking means following rules, but not rules of being, not transcendental rules, but the rules for playing a self-determined game. is the house at 19 kundmanngasse perhaps also the place of the language game?

in fact haus wittgenstein does not derive from any rule in the sense of a canon, a code of function or of aesthetics. it emerged from itself. on the one hand the effect it makes is very ordered, very regular, for instance in the arrangement of the windows, and yet again very free and self-determined, as in the arrangement of the interpenetrating cubes.

let us play a language game. what is there in haus wittgenstein that is determined by "use"?

the house is a social and cultural meeting-place. for this reason a structure of rooms that open up and can also be divided again is created, the hall, the salon, the concert hall and great dining-room, all transparent and capable of being closed, with two terraces in front of them.

these terraces are protected from outside view by a transverse section of the building placed in front of them, and open up the meeting area into the park. the arrangement is free, there are no axes to determine a spatial sequence. it is irregular, but has clear relationships. any schematic approach, for example following the aesthetic doctrine of classicism, would contradict the principal purpose of an open and moving event, namely that of being a social meeting-place.

the rooms are simply rooms. there are no distracting pieces of furniture or pictures. what appears in front of the white walls is the guests, the hosts, their person, their figure, their shape, their gestural language. an additional feature is that rooms that are white and only white have light, light as an autonomous quality. in colourful rooms it is swallowed up by the colours. it is only in white rooms that light remains a quality in its own right.

the windows, door-frames and mountings wittgenstein made in metal, as in an industrial building. the area of glass becomes large in relation to post-frames and bars.

the door handles are nothing but instruments to grip, bent pieces of tubing. taking no account of tradition, which had hitherto made every door handle in the history of architecture into an aesthetic object, an *objet d'art*.

the bearers do not have capitals. there are also no composite beams above them that would have to be supported on a slab. the joists are continuous. thus the bearers can even taper at the top, as in industrial buildings.

the house is asymmetrical. the outer dimensions are derived from, are the result of, the size of the interiors.

in the course of the design process it became clear that more room would be needed in the kitchen and pantry area. so an extension was added. it has a pitched roof, even though the house otherwise has flat roofing, because the extension has tilting windows. windows of this kind cannot be made weatherproof if they are flat.

the size of the windows varies according to whether they are intended for access to the open air, whether they are intended to admit more light to living rooms and reach right down to the floor or whether they belong to bedrooms. wittgenstein made a mistake only in the choice of windows for the upper staircase. they turned out too big, but apparently people were getting tired of the many changes he kept making during the building period.

he entered the lottery to see whether he could win enough money to be able to change things.

it is clear that use produced a series of solutions.

but it is the windows that force us to ask a second question. what is "ordered" in this building? In what does its "rule" lie?

it lies precisely at the point at which it fits in with the criteria of use. it is precisely the arrangement of the windows that gives the building an almost immoderately ordered, almost classical character.

the principle of their sequence goes almost as far as being schematic. the bar division of the windows is almost the same throughout, with vertical articulation. but where just one type of window is assumed, there are in fact eight, even if they occur with varying degrees of frequency. the sequential principle is strict for verticals as well as horizontals. the proportions are fixed.

the parts of the building, even though they differ in volume and each one interpenetrates others differently, appear very ordered. it is a different order from that of the windows. wittgenstein often uses concepts like relationship, family likeness. the cubes behave like relations. they are only similar, but nevertheless make up a unit.

for wittgenstein language always has different aspects. a chess board can be seen in quite different ways, as a whole, as mainly black squares, as mainly white squares, as primarily a diagonal arrangement, as primarily a square arrangement, as a structure of rules for rook, pawns, king or knight. every time we think and we see differently.

it is even the case that the harder we look at something the less we see; if we look carefully at the leaf of a tree we no longer see the tree. if we look at the pattern on a terrazzo floor that contains two figures, a square and a circle, we can see either the circle, or the square. the harder we look, the more exclusive the eye becomes.

thus haus wittgenstein shows different aspects. it has a use dominant and an order dominant, it has

additive order and reductive order. it consists of parts. it is a unit. according to what question we ask, the way we play our language games.
wittgenstein himself never described his house. we have only one little remark about it, the one about "sensitivity and good manners". i think that the house entered his philosophy as a fundamental experience, not as a case of application.
perhaps in this house he not only had experience of what he later called "use", language game and rule. perhaps it was there that he used the words for the first time as key words for his later thinking. haus wittgenstein as the birthplace of his different, second philosophy?
that would suggest itself, as wittgenstein saw use as work that releases something. use is not the practice on the other side of theory, as the whole of the western world sees it. use is itself cognition. use does not release something internal, a core, a value, a truth. we find truth in the act of using. the converse is the case: knowledge is the reverse side of making, of acting, of doing, of use. it is a result, not a guideline.
it seems that wittgenstein only experienced this new philosophy because he was an architect for a time and for a period acquired building as a life-form. he found a new view of things in building and learned, as he said, how things are to be seen.
thus the house at 19 kundmanngasse would be an introduction to a principle of finding order in use and therefore instigating language games.

6 looking

if we understand wittgenstein correctly he refused to take his house to pieces analytically and to deduce it as a logical sequence. he could not abide meta-languages. he recommends language games on the plane of looking. he wants us to produce pictures. just as we should look at sentences, instead of thinking them through.
it is important to know that wittgenstein, even in the *tractatus*, was faced with the question of what is recognition and what is looking. he amazed the world when he distinguished between what can be recognized, what can be said and what is revealed. there are things that are revealed. they are mystical. and he says that anyone who has understood his sentences

must climb out over them as if on a ladder and leave them behind.

for me the striking thing here is the peculiarity of a family home derived from commerce, the steel business and engineering achievements, but also a home where brahms went in and out. wittgenstein was interested in frege and mörike.

the insight that there are things that only "reveal" themselves is very strongly present in early wittgenstein, apparently in the awareness of needing to provoke the naïve positivism that he saw flourishing and expanding everywhere, even in the wiener kreis. this insight remains in late wittgenstein, it even grows. it is a differentiation like that between analoguous, seen thinking and analytical, digital thinking.

analytical thinking can follow only one thread, only one aspect. it has no landscapes in front of it, it does not see, it does not look. and so things revealed remain concealed.

and is this too an experience that is fixed, confirmed and justified by building a house? perhaps wittgenstein had learned that pursuing things that reveal themselves does not point beyond the world, to the mystical, but that the first step even in building a house is looking. and thus he later says even about langauge: if you have sentences in front of you, "don't think look". this could only be said by someone who has learned to trust his seeing, to build on his looking. and this quite literally, by building.

appendix

margarethe stonborough had to emigrate to the united states. during the second world war the house became a red cross military hospital, later a centre for soldiers returning from the war. then margarethe stonborough came back again and lived in the house until her death in 1958. after this it was sold, and was to have been pulled down in 1971, to make room for a highrise hotel. preparations were made and all the trees in the park were cut down. but demolition was stopped at the last minute. there was vigorous protest. a viennese architect found a saviour in the hour of need, who was prepared to buy the plot. this was the ambassador of the then people's republic of bulgaria. he renovated the house and established the cultural department of the embassy there as an open house that is also accessible to visitors who come in memory of wittgenstein.

wittgenstein was sceptical about the development of the world. it would have fitted in with his views if the house really had been pulled down. the fact that it is still standing might – "perhaps" – contradict him.

planning and control

a word came to our assistance almost at the last minute. we all thought that the world could be planned, that the future could be made. the early years of this century overflowed with major planning enterprises like canals and railway. middle-class enterprise may have lost its self-confidence in the 1929 world economic crisis after black friday. but roosevelt's new deal overcame the weakness of a progressive society by state regional programmes for industrialization on an almost global scale. and before lenin made his fellow-countrymen a present of communism he promised them that russia would be electrified. one of the largest dams in the world was built in dnepropetrovsk and the tennessee valley became a model regulated river region, a river state, in which the struggle against soil erosion was as important as providing electricity for rural households. aluminium works were established in the tennessee valley, and later, in the second world war, they began to produce the air fleets that brought america supremacy over half the globe. hitler's struggle against economic collapse consisted of a national motorization programme, mass production of a people's car and building a network of motorways that covered the country. following this model, he then went over to producing armoured scout cars, artillery and dive bombers.

and so the world as a world that could be made was not in the first place one for politicians and economic organizers. it had come into being in the minds of futurists, constructivists and suprematists.

the sky was no longer the home of moon and stars, but of airships and aeroplanes. even trains introduced a new factor for mankind: speed. at first people travelled at 100 kilometres per hour, aeroplanes pushed it to 200, to 500, to 1000. electric lifts made it possible to build blocks of flats of more than eight storeys in the cities. skyscrapers came into being, and with le corbusier's "plan voisin": cities of towers soaring into the skies. manhattan grew like a crystal.

mussolini learned the new age first of all in avant-garde art, before he drained the pontine marshes, the new city emerged in drawings by sant'elia, garnier and hilberseimer. malevich discovered space before the continents were connected by scheduled flights or rockets had been launched. the century became one of a future that could be planned and made. intellectuals turned their backs on salons and secessions, and even the conductor of a symphony orchestra jumped into his sports car and flew his plane himself. the world was portrayed in painting as one of geometrical and technical abstraction. duchamp refused to carry on being an expressionist. he wanted to abandon bourgeoisie and its art, he did not use canvas any more but machinery.

when roosevelt broke his flight to yalta to stop in saudi arabia he offered ibn saud an army of engineers who could irrigate the desert, because there was water if you drilled deep enough. ibn saud declined. the new deal engineers originally came from army pioneering schools. the irrigation systems in california and tennessee needed a different, large-scale, completely systematic approach to thinking, a different one from industrial engineers. and ibn saud was concerned that the engineers who came to make the desert green could be from standard oil. and indeed, these were the very ones who came to the near east. irrigation was no longer of interest, and both roosevelt and stalin neglected their planning programmes and turned their attention to dividing up the world in a different way. opening up the earth was left to businessmen.

planning is a concretized, targeted projection method. development programmes are applied rationally. the new age began when thinking became mathematical. in physics the universe was understood as a system, as celestial mechanics. chemistry was rational architecture of natural building bricks. 18th century enlightenment became concrete in the 20th century in the form of bulldozers and excavators. the way in which aristotle still saw the world, moved by a prime mover, the way in which st. thomas aquinas understood the world order, designed by a planning god, the way in which descartes understood nature, as a machine, this now became true, not just in people's heads, but in the substantial movement of masses, in the production of forces and the intelligence of drawing boards and working organizations. the fact that thinking and the spirit of order allowed themselves to materialize in large-scale technology was a new culture, in which logical conclusions, rational deductions and speculative programmes become concrete in life, in a made and shaped society. as yet, industry was not producing slag heaps, chemistry was not endangering the balance of nature, food was not poisoned, cars did not produce dust and skid-marks, or harmful substances. water was still pure and the forests healthy. the age sounded like a new world model, the model of a new world. it became possible to realize the world as it could be thought out, as it could be designed. transmission meant system, meant method, meant principle, the future meant prognosis. the mathematicization of thinking did not lead to thought chains, but to the active linking of surface dimensions. the logistics of the surface state were established. thought structures became spatial planning. thought laws led to programmes and programmes became function-structures. the night-watchman-state became a law-machine and developed sets of laws with the completeness and automatic quality of a technical laboratory. conclusiveness was the mechanics of the administration and planning also penetrated into provision for life. even families were arranged according to plan. it had been known since the time of keynes that economic processes develop on a cyclical pattern, and so state income and state expenditure were subjected not just to practical reason, but to global planning. and wittgenstein, who was a friend of lord keynes, was working on a definitive version on the structure of logic. he even considered moving to the soviet union for a time.

a fever of optimism broke out. intelligence took on sportive features, the world ultimately acquired overall perspective, was seen in the way in which it had been seen since at the beginning of the modern age, from the renaissance of painting. it acquired vanishing points towards which anything and everything ran. for hitler this meant war, using means that were not just different, but final. what could then be discerned behind this final planning was a system of registration, of transport, of killing camps for "unworthy life", for other races, other convictions. it was planned death.

what was the ultimate answer? what was the triumph of technology? was that the constraints of calculation, of logical connection, of conclusions drawn according to the laws of nature and science?

then we started all over again. the cities that had been destroyed were a new challenge to planning, to systematic building, to rebuilding with the vanishing point of a society at peace. one city model followed another. there was the organic, green city following the idea of the english garden city. the charta of athens and the ciam congresses separated city areas on a basis of living, work and recreation. there was the car-friendly city with junction-free traffic arteries. there was the neighbourhood movement, structuring the city according to the size of school districts. but under the cover of the planning models the cities were destroyed for a second time, they were laid waste by rampant, space-greedy industrial estates, shopping centres and road systems. cities degenerated into a civilization of petrol stations and department stores.

education was seized by a wave of planning. reforms and systems fixed the need for educational quotas, the number of school-leavers. training became a machinery of different institutions, different planning, different examination filters and differently organized courses. the minister of culture ran one of the largest planning institutions and extended the planning principle that was once restricted to the highest echelons of the prussian army right down to what people were supposed to read and think.

in the mean time, planning has faded out again. we have to devote almost all our energies to repairs. as we have now come to know, the world is entirely open to destruction in a number of ways, and that is true here and today, at every moment, and we have become incapable of moving entirely decisively against even one of these kinds of death, whether it be nuclear war or climatic change.

but this is not the main thing to have changed the situation. we are still inclined to prefer to follow the causal chain of reason rather than to perceive damage. if necessary we are prepared to accept the end of the world provided that it is necessary in terms of thought. that is how holy the rationality of the pure method propounded by descartes had become for us.

what changed the situation in reality is the insight that the world, nature, time, development, history do not follow any logical principle. the world is structured completely differently. the world has neither world reason nor a world plan. the legality of the world, of nature, of history can only be established in retrospect. then it is logical because there is and always has been a cause for things that are. but we do not know what cause will affect what will happen tomorrow. do we know who we will be tomorrow?

the word that came to our assistance and that shattered causality as a chain for the future as well is the concept of control.

even if the smart-alecks will say that this concept has always existed, it has only existed as an explanation of the world since the second world war, or more precisely since the days of norbert wiener. at that time biologists, mathematicians, behavioural researchers and physicists got together to think among other things about how an air defence missile could be built that directs itself to its target, that controls itself. little technical models came out with names like "mouse" or "cat", and they were able to demonstrate self-regulation. cybernetics was born, and with it the computer age. "cybernetics" means the science of control. the concept, introduced by norbert wiener in 1948, is derived from the greek word for a helmsman.

a shipping company can draw up as many plans as it likes for its ships' routes, but it is only possible to get from southampton to new york with a helmsman, with a captain. and with the helmsman a new kind of reason arose. conclusive reason, that tries to get on to the track of the general, is replaced by comparative, analogous reason. the causal chain is replaced by feedback, by the self-correcting closed cycle. necessity is replaced by evaluation and judgement. feedback is learning from doing. analogous thinking is comparison derived from making, from doing, from acting.

no ship can travel straight without being steered. no car can hold its direction without steering, and even parents cannot bring up their children without aims and objectives. steering and control are needed according to situation and case. and everything, as good as everything, exists as a situation, a state of affairs, a case. the world is neither ordered being nor mechanical clockwork. it is developing, it is in flux, and has to control its power influences, its dynamics, to find its balance and hold its course.

from plato to kepler the world was perceived as a structure of idealized geometrical bodies one inside the other, as a space of stabilizing proportions with spherical covers and rank orders of ideality. even in the first century b.c. the movements of the stars, of the planets, of the sun and moon were being depicted in mechanisms involving interconnecting toothed wheels. then about 1300 the clock came along, and became a primal image of world mechanics until the time of the enlightenment, where everything is reduced to celestial mechanics, but even down to hegel and marx, who also perceived social processes as interlocking mechanically. it was thomas hobbes in leviathan who was the first to interpret the state as a perfect piece of clockwork.

originally the clock was a rotating lever, certainly developed from the hoist mechanisms used in church building, provided with a weight working on an axis. but then it was also considered to be a thought model for cosmic forces as well and served rational thought, which was a distinctive feature of the middle ages to a large extent, despite other interpretations, as a fundamental experience. the first clocks showed the time of day only incidentally, they were in the first place astronomical devices that made the prime mover almost sensually intelligible. kepler wanted to prove the existence of god from the regular movement that shows that the cosmos is a clock mechanism.

today we increasingly understand nature and world as fluid systems that represent chaos by the standards of digital logic and that like the weather can be predicted only for short periods. nevertheless they are balanced, consistent and reliable, even though they are not subject to any compulsion. we know that a drop of rain on the roof-ridge can run down in one direction or the other. it is not under any compulsion. living nature in particular is indeterminate to the extent that only birth and death are fixed data. between them is life, characterized by sets of circumstances, as a self-determined balance in the field of equilibrium of one's own life-space and life-environment. order can be imposed, but is not given. all that is given is the naked individual in his environment.

this is definitely not to say that reason is an invalid means of giving space to his life. more nietzsche is being read than ever before. will as a life force is a popular argument against enlightenment, reason, planning and rationality. but the world is not sick of too much reason, but of the wrong kind of reason.

descartes, the father of european enlightenment, proclaimed a kind of reason that eliminated the senses as irritations to pure, clear, conclusive thought. anyone who thinks in the same way that we carry out operations with figures can close his eyes and withdraw into an inner world, giving himself over to an algorithm of operational laws. then the signposts determine the direction taken, and not the driver. laws of thinking are axioms, positions or even transcendental definitions, detached from reality. man, who is seen as a being for this kind of thinking, is actually a cripple, he would have to strive to become pure mind.

but the crucial thing about a world thought out in this way is that it simply is thought out. even someone who sees it as a thought-necessity and declares it free of contradiction has to admit that someone else could come along and prove an error or discover an omission. science too is a fluid system and does not have a strict behaviour pattern. in the outposts of material, in the case of elementary particles, advance determination even stops in principle. heisenberg's uncertainty principle establishes that the unpredictability of elementary particles, whether they appear as bodies or waves is not a flaw, but inherent in the system.

shifting human existence solely to the mind is a lamentable restriction. we are beings in a biological, a social and a cultural environment. selfadaptation and self-orientation constitute our self, our person. to this end, senses are an essential prerequisite as organs of our first intuitive cognition. the senses are the starting point of the cycle, the correspondence between view, insight, experience and judgement. without the senses, without perception, by the eye in particular, the cycle would be interrupted, feedback cannot flow and analogous cognition would remain without basis. analogous thinking is feedback thinking and cannot exist without observation and examination.

even where the planning concept seems to have a firmly established place, in architecture, for example, it has been shaken. good architecture is no longer planned today, but developed. even a technical product is a product of a development department rather than a planning department. the concept of planning is too all-embracing and is too much based on the notion that matter and material are mere stuff as in the work of aristotle, that the actual being of things lies in their plan, in their abstract form. the concept of development introduces feedback or the closed loop concept into making. according to this there is no thinking without making, no insight without behaviour.

Nowadays a planned building runs the risk of being a schematized building, a building to a recipe. in fact a building evolves, just as medieval houses used to evolve. now a modern building is too complex in its technology and needs, its situation and purpose, for it still to be possible to plan it. there is much too much to be pursued and examined in detail for it to be possible to fix it in one go. admittedly architects who work like artists, who have an idea and for whom production is mere materialization, can manage without development, without feedback, without control programmes. their building is a transcendental notion. they themselves appeal to genius.

feedback also works its way inwards, and makes comparisons with patterns stored in the memory, social and cultural data, stored insights and stored behavioural patterns. but living, up-to-date thinking does not want to rummage around in stores first of all, but to intervene in given reality. visual thinking, the insight that thinks something in seeing and sees something in thinking cannot be cut out of the closed loop of reason, just as little as thoughts can be captured in a type-face without the guidance of a hand.

we also need more reason than ever. living as pleasure, as a personal experience of post-modern rationalism cuts out the world, the world as it is, and withdraws into aesthetic structures, into illusion, into imagination. but so far we have woken up from every dream.

the dimension of thinking will have to be extended if we acknowledge thinking as a method of control, as personal orientation and instruction for action. this will mean that a lot of things will need to be changed completely.

can the state any longer presume to be the supreme planning organ? hegel defined the state as the institution of the general. hegel's state has done a deal with the citizen that it will protect his work and property if in exchange it is permitted to represent the interests of the general. the role of the state in history and its pact with world reason was generally fixed in advance by hegel. this general quality had already been questioned by william of ockham, and it will now become entirely questionable, if we are expected to order reason out of the state's planning service back into the individual and autonomous human being. reason is individual control in the first place, and individual control is individual reason in the first place.

the state is no longer capable of sitting alongside me at the wheel of my car. i have to drive it myself. i am the only institution that can steer it. and i as a steering and controlling being, as a being that makes driving a car possible only in the sense of individual control, am also the subject of traffic regulations, traffic planning and road building programmes.

in the name of the philosophical and pragmatic claim of planning supremacy, in the name of its responsibility for the general, the state has taken it upon itself to let us take part in a system of traffic and services. in reality the converse is true. we do not drive cars thanks to a gesture by the state, however much universality it claims as the last court of appeal for the general. the state cannot drive a car. it is the controlling driver who makes car travel possible, and the state is merely the institution that guarantees road building and traffic regulation. that could also be done by collective discussions between road-users, and is not a fundamental legitimization of the state.

what all this means is that the individual, the citizen, the self-controlling being is the basis of the state's reality. the state has no general, no superordinate commission to plan. where planning is necessary, as in the building of roads, it carries it out as a service, not as an authority. in future planning should be derived from control, and not vice versa.

ultimately this also means that freedom achieves another and more profound legitimacy and is no longer the desire to be able to do, or not do, as one likes. freedom is not a subjective whim. freedom is not the variety of the individual. it is the criterion for individual control upon which all biological, social and cultural systems are based. these systems require rules, but they must be rules that guarantee the autonomy of controlling reason, the freedom of the individual.

in terms of system theory, a pressure group as an agreement between autonomous individuals is to be more highly esteemed than the state itself, to which supreme planning authority is to be granted. here planning is the result of feedback from independently acting individuals. there is no dialectic of freedom and order. order is there to secure freedom, and not vice versa. traffic regulations are a consequence, not a prerequisite of the car controlled by its driver. freedom comes before order.

we are entering a state of individuals. recourse to the general, to what can be planned cannot support us any longer. our crumbling civilization is caving in further if the state begins to define peace, to say how great a burden can be placed on nature, or how large the room for business manoeuvre should be. we are caving in if the state says what it intends to do about dying forests, exhausted soil and land-gobbling commercial architecture. a better future that can be planned no longer has any pull against direct experience of over-exploitation and ignorance about the individual. the state is losing the power of social, economic and cultural perception. it is scrapping itself. its eyes are blind, its hands are too coarse.

the state is incapable of painting a picture, of composing a song, of bringing up a child, of carrying out an operation, of building a house, of growing flowers. it cannot make healthy food, drive a car, not even oil a sewing machine. all these things fall outside the category of planning. more so today than ever.

because the claim to supremacy that the state has linked with its planning and ordering function, by placing the general above the concrete, has led to bloating of the planning institutions and a planning vacuum that it was only possible to sanction by the use of increased powers for surveys, investigations and statistical research. in the mean time the state is choking on its own planning bureaucracy.

only control, not planning carries the principle of economy within it. control is either effective, or comes too late. but planning outlasts time and moment, like everything general. it usually misses them.

the organ of control is usually a modest instrument. the movable rudder on a ship is relatively small. the movable controlling parts in an aircraft are minimal, and even the regulator on the old steam engine used almost always to consist of just a pair of ball-bearings. society and even the state could be controlled with a lot less effort and expense. who begins to think out a new state? who could find organizational forms for a society of free subjects who derive their concept of freedom from the course of their lives and the way in which they control their lives, and do not try to connect it with william tell or andreas hofer? now, this state cannot be planned either. it has to be practised, somewhere where there are free people. it does not arise from a principle or a planning process. it can probably come into being only through initiatives derived from self-regulating, evaluating, comparative, practical reason, through a form of autonomous rationality. autonomous not in the sense of something arbitrary, but in the sense of responsibility for oneself and a new culture of independence when it is a matter of grasping our reality. its characteristics are not so much things transcendental and reasons for being, they are potentially threatening planning by proliferating planning authorities.

freedom is not just a general condition but the exercise of control. only someone who controls can enter the realms of freedom. but planning disposes. it says what should be. control investigates what can be done and constitutes freedom by doing it. there can be freedom only where planning is replaced by control.

Is this a hymn of praise to free enterprise?

it could be seen like that if one is thinking of the individual entrepreneur. but for a long time now it has been marketing departments, planning strategists who have determined industrial production and the economy of sales as well. for a long time the market has not been the regulator of supply and demand. the market makes most people afraid. risk is a dangerous factor, and claims to be eliminated by planning. and the bigger the business the more all-embracing the company planners' attempts to make things safe. but there are individual entrepreneurs who bet on themselves.

indeed, even in places one would never have suspected to be encrusted with planning, in sport, in games, the call has recently been going out for the player-personality. in football today there is only one authority in reality, that of the trainer, who directs, develops strategies, works out game plans. instead of taking opportunities players have to submit to guidelines. they have become toy operators and dream of the old days when they were themselves the actors and determined the flow and wit of the game.

musicians too have fallen victim to the planning authorities. who still knows the names of the people who actually make the music? there is only the orchestra now, and enthroned above everything, the conductor. he knows which music is right for which audience. where would we be if someone did not direct things from above? and it's not just the music has to be planned, but also appearances. when and where the orchestra plays, deployment is part of planning anticipation. a reputation is produced by weighing up the merits of concerts, festivals, recordings and television. the individual in music, the musician, is now merely an object. the first movements against planning are already taking place in orchestras.

but here too we do not know what is in store for us. it may be that the large orchestra cannot be regenerated. perhaps it will die. but music made by a few people is no less music. even if they manage without a conductor. bach did not use a conductor.

control's sphere of action is concrete reality within the perceptible environment. control has the limitations of directness. planning is general and independent of concrete areas of experience. planning holds to the logic of principles.

the consequence of this must be that large areas of the abstract state for which only statistics are sacred will have to die. almost the whole social security system will have to be brought down to a level where it is open to vivid experience, the level of local politics. the greek city state offers more up-to-date stimuli than the roman empire, which was doomed to fall like all empires, including the holy roman empire. the district, the city is a community in which concrete situations can be evaluated, assessed and solved. it is appropriate to the space in which control can think and exist. the omnipotent state as central power is a relic of religions and philosophies based on the fact that ultimately the world principle can be reduced to a point of supreme abstraction. but the world is not a point but an everything. and this everything is ordered by conciliation, by association, by participation. multiplicity produces relations.

in a future state we need no more omnipotent steerers and planners. we could forget state planners today if we took democracy seriously and brought parliament back within its rights. parliament should define the tasks of politics, and civil servants should carry them out. the fact that the converse is true today, that parliament dances to the chancellor's tune, is also a consequence of a planning ideology aimed at what is ultimately valid, at the definitive, instead of agreeing about a line to be taken on the basis of experienced reality.

we have 2.4 million unemployed in the federal republic, that is 9.6 per cent. but in fact these figures say nothing about the actual scope of unemployment in our country. because alongside the two kinds of unemployment that can be surveyed statistically, normal, temporary unemployment, for which unemployment benefits are paid by social security, and long term unemployment for which unlimited benefits are paid, there is a concealed form of unemployment that does not show up in any statistics and is treated as a "case of hardship". there are 3.1 million cases of hardship in the federal republic, for whom local authorities are responsible. if one takes only half the hardship cases for what they really are, unemployment, then the number of unemployed in the federal republic has to be set at 4 million.

of course this cannot be. a federal chancellor would have to announce the bankruptcy of his social, employment and economic policies if these facts were known. consequently unemployment is divided into two classes and one of them is passed on to a lower authority, the local authority, where it no longer appears as unemployment.

there is one good feature of this development. the state is dying at the top. the problem of unemployment is taken down to a lower, local level, where there is more concrete judgement, closeness to problems and a philosophy of control. if local authorities were still provided with appropriate means to solve this problem then more help would be possible with less bureaucracy because there was more insight into concrete circumstances. anyhow the state, the central state is splintering up, partly also because the one or the other of the länder bosses is pursuing better policies than the ones at the top with their long-term view of planning. the bosses of the länder have to deal with things, not principles.

whether such static monsters as central governments die out, as they have already died out in some enlightened countries, will be as important as the question whether large organizations, central powers decline in favour of more vital, smaller organizations in which the guiding principle is not planning, but control. and here the large-scale state has fallen into its first trap by passing care for the unemployed downwards, for reasons of appearances, from the state into the community.

there will always be general things that need to be planned. but the world we have entered does not need planning so much as intervention into critical situations. today there are more questions than answers. we need another kind of reason, one that is in a position to recognize that questions are questions. philosophy has been looking for the general for too long and the state has for too long known what is valid for either of them to be in a position to perceive questions as such.

questions arise from something questionable. but this can be seen from things that are concrete.

development, a concept

the word "development" has two meanings today: a passive one and an active one. in the passive sense "development" means something that happens, that is in store for us without our doing anything about it. in this sense "development" was revalued since the world was no longer understood as created by god, but, since darwin, seen as a development, brought about by the principle of the survival of the fittest.

in the active sense the word "development", particularly in the fields of technology and applied science, is understood to mean the production, the unfolding of a new product. here setting a task and concept are seen only as a way in. the actual work concerns the testing of a model. one consciously entrusts oneself to a closed circuit of experiment, evaluation and modification. one steers towards a result on a basis of experience. the use is the truth.

the former concept of creativity is inadequate. it suggested that one had a plan, an idea, and then that all that had to be done was to realize it.

in fact the converse is true. having a plan means little more than having a programme. the way in which it can be realized is determined only in development, in practical model experiments. matter is more clever than mind. and mind is the best possible organization of matter.

matter is not longer seen merely as amorphous materiality. matter is organized matter and what can be done can only be done according to the conditions of this matter. our intelligence is necessary to hunt down its intelligence.

modern science became possible as a result of the reversal of the chain of proof. at first people looked for a law, usually understood as a logical structure of the world plan, and then proved it by experiment. galilei reversed the principle. first he conducted his experiments, then he abstracted a law. the experiment, which used to have only a confirmatory function, became, planned as an order, the starting-point of science.

in a similar way "development" became the basis of technology and modern industrial production. today a product cannot be planned, it must be developed. the plan has the function only of a general directive. it is much more important, before actual development, to survey the stipulated conditions, usually in the form of a "duty book", then to search for concepts, possible forms and paths. in the actual development phase the authority of the process is carried over to the experiment, the process, the making. one entrusts oneself to the facts, which admittedly always come out according to the way in which we have defined and installed the arrangement of the experiment.

once reason and insight into the laws of the world were placed above things. today things, reality, conditions are placed above insight. thinking develops in the process of realization and development.

no economy can be surveyed in terms of a plan, no car can be developed in terms of a plan, no social programme can be determined from above, no medicine can be designed on the drawing board.

development is the spirit of below. the modern world likes to be seen as the world below. education is education from below, from the point of view of the children. the state is the state from below, from the point of view of the citizens. the church is the church from below, from the point of view of the sinners. economics is economics from below, from the point of view of the workers and consumers. and mind is mind from below, from the point of view of making.

it is clear that the concept of "development" has no smaller a philosophical dimension than the concept of "being". and yet "development" does not take up a counter-position to "being" in the sense of active production. heraclitus took up a counter-position in the passive sense of the word to beingphilosophy by saying that everything is in a state of flux. he meant that the world was to be understood not as static being, but as changing and dynamic.

in this sense, that the world is developing, the word development in its passive sense as well has been raised to be a programme for a whole science, socalled behavioural research. development is deduced from behaviour.

this science has now become so meaningful that it presents its own epistemology and its own philosophy according to which thinking and cognition are bound in with development processes, shaped by development processes and preformed as development processes.

that would be too little for me. i take the word in its second, its active sense. here development does not simply mean accepting a historical result, but an attempt to find something new. you risk a hypothesis, make a design and check whether they will work by testing them. but testing is not just a check, it provides a challenge to vary the concept constantly. it leads to new paths and usually new results. development is a making process with constantly new thought-results.

the german word entwurf (design) comes from werfen (to throw), and so implies that design is concerned with throwing something out from oneself. in the same way that you throw out a line. the word catches the idea pretty precisely. you throw something up in the air to see how it behaves.

that is something fundamentally different from investigating natural laws, following their logical steps and forming judgements accordingly. this was how classical philosophy saw itself.

development in the active sense needs all one's understanding and intelligence, but the fixed point is not logic, but the model. model situations are designed, models are built and the model shows whether the approach is correct, whether new questions come up that can be answered by new models. logical insight is replaced by insight gained from trial and error, although it should be observed that without the intelligent ability to set up an experiment it is not possible to make mistakes. experiments have to be invented.

why are we in fact content to understand darwin's theory of evolution only in the passive sense of the word? the world is as it is because the fittest survive, he says. but is the world not as it is because nature makes designs, invents models, tests hypotheses?

the diversity of the world does not seem to me to be a remnant of selection struggles allowing the fittest to survive. i should not be surprised if the world were to turn out to be an infinite series of models that admittedly were always tried out and then thrown away or accepted. but without a range one cannot make a choice. one can only reject or accept what is offered as a solution. there is only a better one if there are alternatives at all.

i think that nature plays games. it is not necessary to believe in the handing down of acquired abilities. it is also possible to argue that the world progresses by nature playing, making models that are then presented for testing. then the world would develop not only in the first, the passive sense of the word, but in the second, active one. the world would be one that offers alternatives, presents designs, builds models, produces development. but this is a hypothesis.

be that as it may, the concept of "development" in its active sense contains an entire philosophy like the concept of being in parmenides and that of becoming in heraclitus. but before a thinker takes it over, it needs a phenomenology.

what happens when we develop? the word is only a few decades old in its active sense. we are only just beginning to be aware of the matter.

an apple

it may be its round shape, or its colour, or its mythological significance that makes us see an apple as a complete object, balanced, singular and with a great deal of authority. an apple is a favoured object, a thing. we see things as something significantly more important than conditions, processes, facts. things have individuality and substance, they stand for themselves. that is why thoughts about the world were always thoughts about things in the first place, thoughts about what actually is. philosophy was being philosophy, ontology. the cosmos was populated with beings and things. the war-cry of phenomenology as a philosophical programme was: back to things.

but what is an apple? it is a product of a tree. the tree made it grow. so we must ask the tree if we want to know what an apple is. the tree produced it. why did it produce it? so that the tree can distribute seeds better than by just letting them drop from the branches. the apple is a trick, a trick that makes it easier to spread seeds around.

the whole point is the little black pips inside, the tree's seed. the tree covers these pips with sweet, colourful fruit that animals like to eat. in this way the pips pass through the animal's digestive system and reach some quiet place, well away from the tree's own sphere of influence. the tree develops, almost as though it had thought about it, an attractive product, attractively coloured and attractive to eat, in order to distribute its seeds. the tree, if we ask it, doesn't want the apple as something that is, but as destruction, as something to eat.

seen in this way the apple is just a stopping point, an intermediate stage in a longer functional context that begins with blossom and ends with a stored and fertilized pip. the apple is a stage in a chain of metamorphoses serving a single functional principle, processing the seed.

if you're trying to teach someone to count or even if you're trying to introduce someone to the theory of numbers, apples come into it again. an apple is so unambiguously well-balanced, self-contained, that it can stand as a symbol for an autonomous and singular object, which is an essential feature of counting. teachers still talk about apples when they want to explain addition and subtraction. counting begins when we recognize apples as individual objects and can tell them apart from each other. a single apple is identical with the number one. counting begins with the harvest. we have three, seven or twelve apples. the single apple, the one, is cause and element of counting.

but this one is deceptive. in reality it is not a unit. is is a single phase in a longer process of transformation. an apple grows, ripens, takes on colour and should be devoured as quickly as possible as easily digestible food.

it is not wrong to see an apple as an unambiguous single object, but it is also not wrong to see an apple as a link in a chain of functions, intended to lose its being as quickly as possible.

it's all a case of how you look at it, which means that we deliver the frame of assessment that determines whether the apple is seen as a being or a process.

in 1967 the french mathematician benoit mandelbrot, who lives in the united states, brought up the question of how long the coast of england is in the magazine science. even if the question seemed appropriate to england's coastline in particular, it seemed essentially harmless. the best thing would be to get hold of a good map and work your way along the coastline. but then the question very quickly crops up of whether you should work your way through every little bay. that could easily double the distance. essentially you would have to work your way along the curves of every pebble. how long is the coast of england really? a coast is not a straight line, it has corners. and the more closely you look at it, the more corners you see. mandelbrot developed a new branch of mathematics from this, the mathematics of fractals, of broken corners.

it is clear that it is impossible to give the length of the english coast. there is no correct answer. you can come to an agreement at a conference and give a practicable value, but it can never be precise. the value is a question of interpretation, the conceptual frame that i as a human being put over the facts. how am i supposed to understand the concept of a coast?

an apple can be a symbol of the number one. but it can also serve as a symbol of the number nought: is is intended to be eaten, to be destroyed. the apple is a symbol of self-destruction. according to the way in which it is considered.

the problem turns around. ultimately we cannot ask what an apple is. we have to ask how we think. obviously it is our thought patterns that determine the answer we come up with. it is the nature of our conceptual framework that says how the answer will come out, corresponding to the concepts that we have at our disposal.

for numbers mean nothing to a tree. comparing one apple with another from the point of view of numbers is pointless. each apple is different, is in itself a carrier of the life principle that is concentrated in the pips. colour, the degree of ripeness, the place in which it lies in the grass are the crucial factors for the question of which animal carries it away, far away, as far as possible.

if there is a kind of mathematics that the tree might be interested in it is topology, which manages without numbers, it is a mathematics of positions and conditions.

numbers are not very helpful in explaining chains of function, processes and sequences. but nevertheless why distinguish one apple from another? this is legitimate for as long as we are aware that numbers represent a conceptual framework that does not occur in nature. it is permissible to see the apple as an object that is an example for all things, as the object of objects, as something being in itself, if we are aware that its purpose is to destroy itself, to lose its being.

classical thinking had the weakness that it was insufficiently complex. they clung on to things as things, to apples as apples. they were not able to interpret phenomena as a sequence, as elements in a series of developments or as knots in a series of interconnections. the concept of the object was determined by duration, isolation, individuality, singularity and natural autonomy. an object was determined by itself. it defined itself in terms of itself.

and so right down to the present day a building is seen as an object that one plans and erects and then sees as complete. it has the autonomy and isolation of a work of art, that is complete when it is complete. it is difficult even for modern architects to see a building as an item of practical use that derives its form from its function.

being-thinking can also be seen in religions. god is creator of a world that is complete, he is the creator of an object world. but what if the world started with a function, just as the apple gained its form and its substance from a programme of seed multiplication and storage. there would not be any apples if animals did not eat and distribute them. modern thinking is connection thinking, is awareness of fields and perception of involvements. accordingly structure has taken the place of form.

for almost anyone a wine bottle is a form-restricted object in the first place. it is as autonomous as an apple. it is not the result of a programme.

let us establish a brief: we're looking for an object in which to store wine. it should
- contain enough for an evening,
- have an opening from which it is easy to pour,
- but it should be possible to close it again,
- be usable with one hand,
- show how much wine is left,
- be stackable and capable of storage,
- not take up too much room on the dining table,
- protect the wine from the light.

and what does this give us? a wine bottle.

the formally beautiful object suddenly becomes a functional intersection point, the knot that combines and sums up the most various demands coherently. the result is the sum of functional demands. think of constructivist painting, of braque, of gris, of ozenfant, of picasso, or think of the favourite object for drawing lessons, the bottle is a primeval model of good form. in its variations and the completeness of its shape it is again a *ding an sich*. in truth it is the result of its functions. it is fulfilment of purpose.

here the difference between design and art can be discerned. in the classical world of object thinking the artist was a creator of isolated works. but in design it is a matter of the objective definition of facts, the summing up of demands and the discovery of a result.

design is concerned with the dimension of use, of fulfilment of function, of application programmes. things take on the character of tools, they are there for processes, they prove themselves in the sequence of demands and purposes. works of art are complete. they can be parked in museums. design is not particularly suited to collections. it proves itself in daily use.

an apple is a symbol of one and of nought. design too can pass away, destroy itself in use, even if it was designed as the best possible product.

something quite ordinary

1
as long as there is part of society that has a say there will be opera. opera is a secular church that celebrates high mass in honour of special people, namely people who have a say. the ladies and gentlemen meet, wearing their finest clothes and housed in expensive architecture, even if it has to be on a working day at half past four in the afternoon, as for the wagner festival in bayreuth.
opera is about special people, and so special people not only go to it, they put up with it. it does not hurt them to celebrate even heroic kitsch so long as it confirms their greatness and significance.
richard wagner even gave heroes religious traits. what is special lives in the cosmos, in fate, in tragedy, in myth. admittedly religion is no longer the astonished apollonianism of ancient athens, but that of the valkyries and wotan, corresponding with the figure of the upper-middle-class factory owner, enthroned in *villa hügel*. capitalist enthusiasm for work born of a calvinist religion of virtue, creative power and the reprehensibility of idleness, as described by the muchquoted max weber, has become a religion of power and strength. if spinoza or kant had ever passed across the bayreuth stage they would have been laughing-stocks for ever after, so gigantic were the singers personifying the new heavens. the orchestra now played fate. anyone emitting the sounds of the cosmos had to have a massive chest, even physiologically speaking.
why did nietzsche quarrel with wagner? ultimately he is the prophet of the special per se, the prophet of the superman. and he had once said of wagner's music: "that is heaven on earth." when near wagner, nietzsche had felt "near the divine": wagner was the fusion of nature with art, fulfilment of life through art. real life unfolded in the galleries of art, in the halls of music. one was raised up into the sounds of aesthetic transfiguration, and one's own life changed in the current of aesthetic sensation and imagination. religion, lost in the bourgeoisie, appeared in the new garb of art, in redemption through sensations, through the enjoyment of art.
nietzsche, who once wanted to write an opera himself, honoured wagner as a new prophet and proved to

be an ideological forerunner: he poured the malice of narrow-mindedness that was unfit to live, if not life-despising, over precise thinking, analytical criticism and enlightenment. nietzsche provided the philosophy for the appearance of art per se.

and yet he broke with wagner. he included wagner in the reassessment of all values. ultimately he did not want life to depend on art, to allow it to be absorbed into art, but he wanted to make life itself an art. life should itself be a subject of art, instead of being sacrificed in art and lost in the consecration of the aesthetic. art too can cause sickliness.

nietzsche pushed creativity a stage further, each to be the artist of himself. but art continued to be defined as special and out of the ordinary, the ego had to become a super-ego.

richard wagner had entered the lists against the way in which opera was pieced together from a selected, more or less incidental text with music added on. he wanted the gesamtkunstwerk, a unity of text, music and setting, as significant art. the romantic demand for unity of life, convictions and aesthetics is clear. life becomes life through art, and art has no other meaning but life. this should mean that there was no more religion outside art. religion had to become part of opera, along with the newly-created state, the newly-created nation, together with its history, its people, its myth. wagner had even managed to expand this unity of history and religion, of verbal art and music to include architecture, with the festspielhaus, which advanced to be a temple in the annual celebration of the festival and its congregation.

nietzsche could not stand this in the long run. he had only with difficulty freed himself from christianity, and equally from the prussian state, although he had volunteered to serve in the war of 1870. he could no longer be asked to bow to princes or fall to his knees before christianity.

in wagner's villa in tribschen near lucerne there were once two rooms permanently at the disposal of nietzsche, the young professor from basle. then when wagner went to bayreuth and put on *tristan* the physical distance also confirmed inner cooling off and separation: wagner was populating the stage with false types, suffering from an inner sickness, he was running after redemption, making psychology into art, and life merely into a play. "the artist will soon be seen as a splendid relic", said nietzsche. he despised show, fuss and false inwardness.

anyway, nietzsche could imagine humanity without artists, which actually is still not possible today.

for nietzsche the human being himself became a great work of art. only someone who makes himself into a work of art, who finds "the great style", who explains himself from himself is a human being. "i teach you of the superman. man is something that should be overcome." art is something special, and became unique.

nietzsche had heard lectures by jakob burckhardt about the great men of the renaissance and moved in a milieu in which genius was worshipped, including machiavelli. his main work was originally to be called "*the will to power*". in reality he wanted more. in the days of his collapse in turin, at new year 1889, he signed himself "the crucified".

an aesthetic existence was too little for him, and so was an historical one. he wanted to be a redeemer. the need to redeem was more than "great style" or lonely will. life as a work of art should lead to life as redemption, endowing religion and congregation.

nietzsche was opposed to socratic questioning and thinking, analytical and enlightened criticism on the one side. it strangled life, the expression of life and the life-will. on the other side was christianity, which humbled the individual into being a virtuous member of the herd, made him small, ordinary.

nietzsche sought historical and scientific access to the renaissance and to antiquity. he himself lectured on the pre-socratics. but he saw christianity only in a polemic against the protestant environment of his youth and the religious practices of his time. he never wanted to understand it. he rubbed against it in order to reach what he hated about it in his own way. he wanted to become so strong that he could himself forgive.

this has as little in common with true christianity as high mass as a work of art has with the sermon on the sea of genezareth. the great, the special, is precisely what christianity does not want. god is not the jahwe of the hereafter, but a kind of father who turns to the little man, the lost, the sinners.

christianity does not have an historical gesture, at least not originally. it does not want the great and just, not the favourites of the gods, it mixes with little people, tax-collectors, craftsmen and fishermen, with women, even women who sell love, and takes even the single little person as seriously as an individual as the heroes or the great men of history. the unique thing is that it does not seek the unique. it is a religion that is against religion writ large, against high religion, against the high priests. originally christianity knew no priests, no scribes, no churches, no high mass and so also not the drama of forgiveness from above. the reversal of values lies in redirecting the course towards the holy, the temples and the high priests, towards the just, and towards the individual, however small. it is he in whom a god of a new understanding of religion, of a new covenant, is well pleased.

this is another god than the god of the old testament, of the prophets, whether they are called jeremiah, john or even zarathustra. certainly the new testament has been overtaken by the old testament. then there were priests, churches and altars. the simple table in the room of the last supper again became the altar of the holy of holies. tragedy of historical dialectic. but it was not meant like that, you can read it up and check, though unfortunately in words that have lost their content being babbled over so repeatedly.

god as super-father, the angry, punishing, just, rewarding god was in fact dead. the god who has power like emperors and kings, who makes history like warriors and heroes, the ruling god who can only forgive because he is powerful, this god has become an historical element in christianity, but was not its original intention. this god is dead.

nietzsche was not only blind to christianity, he was blind to the democratic and social movements of his period as well, because he saw history as a development of power and the powerful. he simply did not see them. and he was blind as far as christianity was concerned because he saw a god for whom redemption also meant a manifestation of power. he made himself the equal of this god by signing himself "the crucified". he wanted to redeem. but redemption from a religion of super-power had long since taken place. it gave the individual autonomy and freedom by overcoming a religion of the punishing, angry, ever-just super-ego. life as a titanic work of art had been replaced in galilee by a religion of openness and closeness that would not tolerate any domination, any aspiration to power. this was possible because every individual, ever the smallest had become worthy enough and big enough to live his own life and to be recognized in his own life. this meant renunciation of historical distinction as a category of greatness. it meant abandoning creativity at the expense of others. it even meant renunciation of singularity, of dionysiac development at the expense of others. real greatness is perhaps the equality of the anonymous, without expectation of public or historical distinction. life is an achievement, a design, it is work, but not a unique work of art. man tills his field with care, harvests with joy, and that is all. socrates made no demands, he disliked the special. his thinking moved in the realms of modesty.

art is a metaphysics of creativity. a work of art is super-reality, something that does not have to justify, that explains itself. the beautiful transcends the real. it justifies itself. anyone who sees his life as a work of art does not want to find himself but wishes to pass beyond himself. he needs a heaven, the drama of the highest, even if he kills the god whose place he wishes to take.

this was the case until thomas mann, who played the role of the high priest, the keeper of art, in such a way that his children longed for his death.

today the concept of metaphysics means explanation from the outside. things are not explained in terms of themselves, but in terms of a "superordinate" principle. the concept comes from aristotle, and means an explanation of physical reality from general principles. thus movement is a general principle that helps us to understand the world. kant's transcendental categories are also general principles of this kind. that the whole is more than the sum of its parts cannot be proved in physical terms, but it nevertheless seems plausible. that the mind is more than the body also seems certain, but only for as long as one is not obliged to prove its existence as a fact. but mind could also be the organization-form of life, and thus a function of the body, and part of it.

be that as it may, there is a philosophical virtue that forbids explaining something other than in terms of itself. anything that is not explicable in terms of itself, that needs outside explanation, justifies something outside, but does not explain the thing.

things do point beyond themselves. the river we describe suggests a source. nothing is without a context. everything is complex and compels us to think beyond it. but that is different from thinking of a thing from the point of view of something outside, even if we accept that it is superordinated to the thing. it is impermissible to say: the river flows because there is a prime mover. the river flows because water obeys gravity. the fact that there was a prime mover would require there to be two aggregate conditions of the world. the static and the moving. the first movement would then have come from the static one. but what if movement came first, if everything is movement and being static is only a special case of movement, its condition when it reaches zero?

it is possible to speculate that there was a prime mover, but it is not permissible to call upon his assistance when we ask why the river flows.

if a work of art is a metaphysics of the aesthetic, this does not mean that there is no such thing as the aesthetic, and it does not mean that there is no such thing as the artificial, the work, something made. technology exists, language exists, the made thing exists, and the found and invented word exists. culture is precisely about dealing with both, even under aesthetic criteria. but the work of art leaves behind and exceeds this made thing. it wishes to be only itself, and to that extent is metaphysics.

things made as technology and communication, as things and as media, are what they are through design, through the way in which they are shaped, through concern that they should be as good as possible. the criterion of design is use. it is in use that the degree of rightness is expressed. works of art withdraw from rightness. they are no longer susceptible to examination, particularly since they have been released from the function of portrayal. even van gogh's cornfield did not have to be correct. after his break with wagner, nietzsche believed that the music in georges bizet's carmen was better. he saw twenty performances of it. he had no other reasons than those of his inclinations.

art creates signs. but not signs that stand for something, just signs as signs. it is unsemantic syntax. it is like a language that consists only of grammar. but it is precisely that, this weakness, that makes it susceptible to having meanings attached to it, indeed means that meanings are heaped upon it. then it becomes metaphysics.

richard wagner's music is not just music, in fact it does not intend to be music first and foremost. it is world feeling, religion. if it were just style is could be assessed as an examination of music, as a new syntactical model and as an extension of sign repertoires, as an aesthetic experiment. but it is not intended to be that. because it cannot be projected upon a world of reality, because it is beyond good and evil, true and false, it can claim to create a new reality, a higher reality. but only for as long as one is prepared to allow oneself to be abducted from the world in this way.

the fact that there was such a thing as national socialism, the discovery of the people and the nation with a metaphysics of the fatherland and the inevitable consequence that other fatherlands were drawn into wars is a perversion of politics, but says nothing against politics as such. the fact that we live at a time in which the work of art has moved to the highest point of the explanation of existence is again a case of excess, but says nothing against continuing to develop signs, to pursue aesthetic combinations and to look for valid shape. but this has the objectivity and dryness of something like scientific investigation or the achievements of craftsmen. these come to us unburdened with transcendency and the hereafter. the transcendental fatherland brought only death and the transcendental work of art only the spurning of reality, a world full of trash and rubbish.

but precisely because it involves loss of reality, art is prescribed for everyone who suffers from loss of the world and needs compensation. and this is true of all of us. all the victims of industrial production, who are no longer allowed to do their own work, no longer allowed to produce their own products, now longer allowed to travel on their own journeys, no longer allowed to have their own needs, no longer allowed to consume their own consumption, who are fitted into the constraints of the market.

because things are no longer right in the low-lying areas of the world we are pointed to higher ones. in ancient china, in ancient greece images of house gods were hung on the wall, in the middle ages they hung up crucifixes. today we hang up art.

there is a transcendental idealism of the hereafter. according to this, the things of this world are copies of the ideas of a higher world. there is also an immanent idealism, idealization from the inside outwards. something turns into art.

all that is needed is the appropriate celebration, and the profane becomes sacred. art can be made from elementary geometry, from circle, square and rectangle, provided they are put into mounts. something quite ordinary can be idealized, raised to the status of truth if correct presentation is matched with the correct price, the correct market, the right institution and a ministry that protects everything. the 20th century has found its higher being in the worship of art.

2

there was a second 20th century universal demand that corresponded to the demand to live life as a work of art. it was the demand for absolute cognition, which means the same as cognition of the absolute, of the general. it is the demand for absolute clarity.

the physicist understands this as the world formula, the mathematician as logic handled in terms of algebra, the philosopher as a system of thought that cannot be contradicted.

the zeitgeist is a fashion, and where it is in fashion the sentence "everything that can be expressed can be clearly expressed" can be heard everywhere. and this is frequently followed by the sentence "whereof one cannot speak thereof one must be silent." these sentences are by ludwig wittgenstein, from his *tractatus logico-philosophicus*, and are a second motto for our century, alongside nietzsche's "god is dead". wittgenstein has now been canonized in the same way as previously happened with nietzsche and is happening again today in french philosophy. the prophet of clarity is set against the prophet of autonomy.

wittgenstein behaved like a chemist who says: if i know the laws of combination of all the elements i can manufacture any material in the world. if i know all the logical connections that occur in sentences, i can tackle every philosophical problem. what sentence forms are there, what makes a sentence into a sentence, qualifies it as a statement?

the elementary sentence portrays the facts of the world. all elementary sentences present a picture of the world. the tractatus was originally called *der satz*, the sentence, and claimed to solve all problems of philosophy. this sounds surprising. normally philosophy is looking for the cosmic whole, seeks to grasp things in their totality. when a philosopher asserts that he wants to grasp being as being that sounds plausible, but not if he says that he wants to grasp the sentence as a sentence.

but geometry as a whole cannot be described, it can be made with a ruler and a compass. even descartes was concerned not with grasping knowledge but the method by which cognition emerges. nature cannot be described, but the way in which it is organized can. in the same way wittgenstein is turning not to the content, and certainly not the total content of philosophy, but to the method of making statements more truthfully. if we grasp what makes a sentence or sentences we can experience everything that can be said. we have to be silent about everything else.

at first this statement was seen as a reservation about clever chatter suggesting that someone is omniscient. but wittgenstein was concerned with a philosophical problem, and that is, whether statements can be made about things that are not facts, are not concrete. can statements be made about universals?

russell still saw truth as an agreement between statements and facts. for him there really are general concepts.

here wittgenstein does not agree. in his view, general concepts are merely a linguistic expression.

now there are many things that cannot be described as facts. what is the meaning of life? is there such a thing as "love"? there are lovers who love each other, but "love"? something can be said about lived love. something can be said about lovers. wittgenstein wishes to be silent about "love" because every sentence refers to facts and otherwise becomes an unreal sentence. wittgenstein speaks of the facts of the world but not "the" world as a totality. nothing can be said about a totality that does not refer to facts. it is possible to have intuitions. but "intuition is an unnecessary excuse." it is better to be silent, even if the fact is insistent as a phenomenon. the condition of the world can show, but we talk about facts. one can "see" the world in a particular way, but that is not a statement about it. statements refer to facts. it is better to be silent if one can say nothing.

there are statements about facts. their correctness is demonstrated in logic. but there is no such thing as "the" truth. there is clarity. everything that one can say can be said clearly. even if one has otherwise to be silent.

the demand for an ultimately valid statement is a demand for an ultimately valid definition of the logical structure of a sentence. the purest form of rational thought is manifest in this demand.

nietzsche despised analytical thinking of this kind. despised it because it kills life, strangles will.
what many people, even many of wittgenstein's admirers do not know is that he too learned to despise this kind of thinking.
wittgenstein is so captivating because he produced two philosophies, one contrasting with another. he has not left any doctrine behind, but himself provides the example that philosophy is work that can lead to overthrowing something one used to think. as a rule the search for truth makes people vain. they think they have found something special, and make it into a system, a doctrine, a proclamation, if not a gospel. zarathustra himself takes up the language of proclamation. wittgenstein demonstrates the nature of his thinking by revealing his mistakes. his philosophy consists of looking for his own mistakes. it is work, work on cognition, not a message.
we have become accustomed to messages. they promise the fulfilment of life, but also an exit from life. this kind of philosophy is impermissible in the eyes of wittgenstein. life itself is the object of life and thus of cognition.
in his second philosophy, wittgenstein says that he had made significant mistakes. there is no such thing as the ideal sentence that he was looking for as an elementary sentence. logic is not in a position to show people what a correct sentence looks like. it is logic for a vacuum. it is looking for a super-order behind language where every sentence is in order as it is. there is no background that orders everything. he had allowed himself to be blinded by an ideal. logic is just a pair of spectacles. we should take them off.
wittgenstein sees the rigour of logic coming unstuck. language as crystalline clarity is a fiction. it is a prejudice. the whole way of looking at things should be turned round:
we must remain with ordinary language and the things of everyday thinking. we must take langugae as it is. there is no sense in looking for depth in language with the help of logic. precision is not an aim. it does not help us to get to the bottom of things.
there is no point in setting up a theory of thinking. "all explanation must be dismissed and replaced only by description." language and thought are nothing unique. we think in the language of the everyday. "we take words back from a metaphysical use to an everyday one."

163

when philosophers use words like "being", "object", "ego" and try to grasp the essence of a thing one has to ask oneself whether such words are used like this in colloquial language.

if theory is replaced by observation, and logical analysis is replaced by description, then it may seem to many that great and important things, things that are interesting, are being destroyed. "but it is only castles in the air that are being destroyed."

now it should not be thought that wittgenstein is smashing up the great philosophies of the world and the philosophies of greatness and depth only to found a philosophy of his own. the following statement refers to himself: "the results of philosophy are the discovery of some plain nonsense and bruises that understanding has acquired by running up against the borders of language." "the aspects of things that are most important for us are hidden by their simplicity and everyday quality." "when i talk about language i have to speak the language of every day."

and where does language become accessible? in use. "understanding a sentence means understanding a language. understanding a language means mastering a technique." philosophy is a practice. language as such is dead. what gives it life? use. where an arrow is pointing is not implicit in it. it is revealed in use, in application.

can one sense that worlds are collapsing here? that mountains and hills are being laid low, and valleys exalted? the essence of things is reduced to the everyday, the general to the concrete, the special to the perfectly ordinary and the profound to the superficial, being to use. an iconoclastic moment for western culture?

can one see that in wittgenstein? taking the superhuman back to the most human? one can, because in doing it he is criticizing himself. for it was he who had demanded ultimate clarity, the solving of all the problems of philosophy.

is he leaving nothing behind but fragments of stone and rubble? wittgenstein asked himself. no, he was only destroying castles in the air. "we are opening up the ground of language on which they stood." in the language of every day.

3

wagner wanted to give fulfilment to life in art. art should take life away and give it new content. nietzsche did not want to take away. he declared his own life to be a work of art and lived it as artistic creation, as great style. down to the second crucifixion.

in the mean time art has been so stigmatized and sanctified that everything connected with it becomes noble and holy. even business. if business, business with oil, business with chemistry, business with money is declared a work of art, associated with an artist, presented as a performance, then it is raised into the realms of culture. business art as art business. this is art after picasso. andy warhol created it.

art and life are a contradiction today. art is a raising, an idealization beyond life. it points to the other. art is the metaphysics of the aesthetic, just as the sacred is the metaphysics of the moral. it is raised, and is honoured and worshipped in museums in just the same way as the holy in the holy of holies, in churches and temples.

when life loses its meaning a new meaning is installed, that of the hereafter. if one no longer knows why one is bringing up children, no longer knows what one is working for, no longer knows whether other people's products are good, if one no longer knows whether words are true, whether food is still healthy, then perhaps all that can help is revolution, radical change, in any case the shift of life expectancy into metaphysics.

if the state integrates its subjects into a closed system, if people are no longer able to live their own lives, then they are promised something better, the fatherland for which it is even worth dying. it is greater, more powerful, more full of content than one's own four walls. it permits a mind that no longer has a goal, a projection. a projection that so glorifies our aggression that we are even prepared to die for it.

glorification is a simple social technique. it has existed for as long as power has existed. power understood generally.

we will even die for cars. it is suggested to us that having a car fulfils the dream of freedom. this dream works wonders. the car industry is still growing. new registrations are peaking. everyone always has to have the very latest model, and then the car industry's economic programme is all right. this is a prosaic concept. but no-one is supposed to know this truth. knowing it would lead to the opposite: people would start to wonder whether they really needed yet another new car.

and so glorification and celebration come in again, the status of the car is raised. it acquires the power of jaguar, cheetah or tiger, it becomes supernaturally beautiful, like a woman. the last goddesses are in the temples of the car business. you put your foot on the accelerator and forget the little, trivial ego that civilization has made of man. you experience freedom.

life forfeits its element of being worth living. as a consequence we glorify ourselves out of it. the working day is tolerable only if there is a service on sunday. your ego gets in its own way, life knots itself into a tangle. it could be untangled. but then man, the subject, the consumer, the believer would be free, he would live himself. and what powers want that to happen?

art is a profane glorification after the sacred has started to lose its luminosity. the less people go to church the more they go to museums. they do not find any less devotion, quiet, inner peace, raising oneself above oneself there. pure colour, pure form is as up-lifting as pure doctrine.

there is no such thing as a pure doctrine, because otherwise there would be hundreds and thousands of them, as many as there are doctrines in the world. but every true believer needs them and is enabled by them to forget himself and die for a pure doctrine, fighting others who also claim to follow pure doctrine.

every religious society is in possession of the truth, and every national state deserves the claim to be honoured alone, every make of car is the best and every artistic movement has superceded all the others.

many great painters at the beginning of this century saw this and thought that they could overcome this dilemma between life and glory. they wanted to help simply to let light into their own huts instead of celebrating a longing for the unreachable stars, as the great art of the bourgeois period had done.

mondrian once wanted to redeem painting from art, and so did tatlin and malevich. warhol too denounced an art that incapacitated man by worship. in protest he turned to the campbell's soup tin, to mass production labels, to design, to the trivial.

no-one could survive in this rarefied atmosphere, in this loneliness. tatlin was the nearest, remaining true to the doctrine that anyone who wanted to give life creativity, design, aesthetics must give up art. the stream of culture could only be diverted in favour of man if he renounced serving higher things and turned to the ordinary. the redeemer must stop being concerned with the just, with saints, and turn to those who have to live the lives of human beings.

all these artists were overtaken by their institution, by art, by the art trade, by museums. and so christianity, which did not intend to be the religion of the high priests, was taken back into the house of god again.

who could be creatively active without selling pictures? who was to create an aesthetic event without the mechanism of the market?

warhol found the most elegant way out. he invented a new genre, "businessart" and the "art-business". he could no longer return to design, to the economic level of an engineer. art manufactured unique things, which were paid for as unique, as originals.

warhol placed advertisements: "come to warhol, he will paint your picture, you will experience a few hours close to art. please bring photo." all this for 35,000 dollars. "business-art" was born. real art, said warhol, is business. even in business creative methods and artistic freedom can develop. an honest soul.

the whole of new york went on a pilgrimage to the new temples. galleries shot out of the ground like mushrooms. people used to write cheques for the social services, for the poor, for the third world, for handicapped children, but now people started to demand this kind of humane service from the state. people's own money flowed into the newly flourishing business art market, which is at the same time art-business. works of art were piled up as investments.

this had the pleasant side-effect that art found its way into safes, disappeared to a large extent and thus the market was always open, unsaturated, ready for the next trend, doctrine, fashion.

in fact it was high time for art also to fit in with the principle of our culture of transferring quality into quantity. this was occasionally misunderstood. there were painters who painted with ruler and compass, to get on to the tracks of the quantity of aesthetic quality. they wanted to work it out. but the principle of our culture sees quantification as portraying all kinds of quality as just one form of quantity, money.

in the field of science and technology, what increasingly count are things that bring in money or have the prospect of bringing in money. so warhol's step of tying art not to some standards or informative sizes and measured values, but to money as money, was disarmingly honest. business-art is not just art that is sold, but money as art, business as art, doing business as an artistic process. business as an aesthetic ritual. earning money as an aesthetic competition.

if even the art trade consists mainly of providing pictures as investments for people who have an idea of business but not of art, then why should painters who have an idea of art but not of business not see works of art as an investment?

what does it matter if one hand steals from another, the process itself can be art, to the extent that it is done as warhol did it. or beuys. or . . . who will be next?

art is no longer beyond business, it is in the middle of it. it is the stimulus of business, business with aesthetic enjoyment, with the aura of culture.

also the act of glorification. "business" in the temple is business in a "temple".

if the world is to die then it will probably choke on business. business legitimizes everything. everything that is business is legitimate. it is all right for every river in the world to be full of pollution if it serves the maximization of profit. all the woods can be cut down or destroyed by exhaust gases if it serves maximization of profit. if war is a business, then wars are permitted too. and killing each other, murdering each other is still a business. business with methods of killing each other.

why does business have to be dirty? why do buildings belonging to groups of companies have to look like offices? anyone who builds with art, who gets involved in art deals, and also does business with art raises maximization of profit to the level of culture. the world has become as ordinary as that.

life is a design. the design of a life-form. we have to take it in hand ourselves, we have seen through the techniques of idealization. neither the fatherland nor the work of art nor "the" truth will help us to live life ourselves. and that means life in an environment, not in the cosmos. it means life within one's own feasibility, not as a work of art. it means life in what is given, not in the general. it means everyday life, not sunday life. it means life as quite ordinary life. it means life as something quite ordinary. the life of our own work, our own surroundings, our own friends and neighbours. it has to be designed. it is design, not art, because the balance of the individual in his field of environment, people and things is not given, but has to be achieved. it has to be manufactured as a life-form of our own, as our own life's work. anyone who lives a real life is making a real creative achievement.

the perfectly ordinary is hard work. and life pays off in the perfectly ordinary. culture develops in the ordinary. as a form that we give to our lives.

life form and ideology

what is truth?
our present understanding is that truth, even in faith, is not definitively valid. truth is the most recently valid position of insight, which has the characteristic feature that older, previous truths have turned out not to be right. truth is the one that is valid know, and it has to permit itself to disappear again as a result of new insights. this is also the justification for "belief in the period".

truth is the best insight at the time. it is insight into the aggregate condition of the best arguments.

there are other aggregate conditions of truth. truth first seems to us like an insight, then a doctrine, a system, it even becomes an (infallible) institution.

a hundred years of workers' movements in their bolshevik form demonstrated all phases of this transition from insight to institution, in which ultimately the believing individual can be condemned to death by an institution guarding the truth, on the instructions of someone who is the person who has truth at his disposal.

the emergence of christianity can only be understood if one understands its counterposition to a truth as doctrine, law and institution, and recognizes the attempt to take correct action back to insight and conscience, to free religion from outside determination resulting in outward action.

christianity did not emerge because a new belief in a new god was necessary, but because faith in the common god was devalued by a religion of outward religious expression. this was reason enough for jesus of nazareth to leave the ship, indeed to go over to the opposition, the underground, and accept persecution.

would there be as much courage in questioning orthodoxy today?

christianity remained within the framework of the religion of the fathers, but protested against the authority of the law. it referred to a god as a father who is father of each individual and creates religion in direct contact with him.

in jewish history the struggle between those who were true to the law against those who were free from the law had already reached a climax 200 years before christ. a jewish religion of enlightenment, a jewish religion of openness to the world rose up against an orthodox outward cult. there was an attempt in jerusalem, particularly among aristocratic families, to expand the religion of their fathers to a covenant with other religions of hellenism and to open themselves up to more rational explanations of the world coming above all from greece. this led to a violent attempt to abolish ritual religious practices like keeping the sabbath holy, circumcision, the banning of various foods and drinks, and general legal provisions in favour of a subjective and rational world religion. all this on the basis of the ethically demanding monotheism of their fathers.

the jews were highly esteemed by the greeks because of their strongly ethically determined belief in one god. they were called the "philosophers". there was interest in them, and the jews as well, particularly in the diaspora, were interested in the greeks. and the story of the prophets also shows the influence of the ancient world. more argumentative books of wisdom appear, finally demanding the abandonment of atavisms like burnt offerings and abolishing a superficial religion of commandments.

immanuel kant once believed that religion would make progress in the age of reason from the pursuit of religious customs to an ethical and rational confrontation with the reason of the world. there had been an attempt to do this by the jews almost two hundred years before christ.

success was not just negative, it led to extreme belief in the thora and a binding of the religious individual to formalized rituals extending as far as burnt and slaughtered offerings. sect-like orders emerged like the essenes, sadducees and pharisees, who tried to retain the heritage as teaching, doctrine as an institution. the essenes were an ascetic elite order that set up the ideal of the "just", the holy jew who came increasingly close to god through faith and religious practice. the sadducees tried to abolish the Greek belief in immortality, and the pharisees presented themselves as zealots, as fundamentalists of the thora, the law, and controlled the pursuit of ritual commandments in an almost statistical fashion.

in contrast with the essenes, jesus took the view that it was precisely not the just that religion should have in mind, but the very least of people, the poor, the sinners, the rejects. god was not seeking to speak to the heroes of virtue, with the saints, but with the lowly. unlike the sadducees, he was of the opinion that only heaven can be a reward if most people have to suffer unjustly. and in terms of the pharisees he not only practised provocative infringements of the requirements of the law, he spoke against the whole grounding of religion in law and justified religious behaviour by motive. motivation determines righteousness, not faithfulness to the law.

in a somewhat threadbare concept, this motivation is called love. today, where this word is pushed to and fro between charity, sexuality, helpfulness and the content of films, including the religious state of the soul and agreeable obseqiousness, it is perhaps more usual to speak of inclination and attention. some speak of solidarity. what is meant is not alien to us: acting and living that is not guided from outside, but motivated by our own attentiveness, our own insight and our own responsibility, stimulated by attentiveness to a god who is himself like a caring father.

religion as doctrine, ideology and institution is faced by religion as life-form. as opposed to the earlier jews, who turned against a religion of following commandments, as opposed to the jewish "hellenists", jesus goes even further. he does not think, like kant for example, of enlightenment, of merely rational self-determination in the sense of liberality, he demands an attitude, because real insight can be acquired only in action that makes a statement. mere evaluation creates only a free and open view. christianity is not a religion of intellectual world-insight, it is attitude and intervention, insight as a result of helping, of involvement.

what jesus wanted can be deduced from what he didn't want. he didn't want scribes, he had nothing written down. he had no priests, he did not stand in front of altars. it was not until constantine that churches were built for christians. jesus had no sacred book, no thora. he did not turn only to the faithful, only to the jews. he preached for the people, he lived among the people. he had no religious place. he lived on hills, in houses, he did not make a single sacrifice to god on an altar. jesus brought people into communion with god themselves, he avoided deviations via a representative institution. he definitely did not see the faithful as members of a sect.

and fundamentally this remained the case until christianity became the state religion in the latter stages of the roman empire and the existing rituals were seen as an ideological support of the state. from the time of constantine onwards priests became officials.

of course modern christianity is not immune from degenerating into a set of teachings, a doctrine, an institution, just as little as the religion of the fathers was immune from this. a religion of protesting prophets and an official religion of the temple as a religious authority runs through the old testament, a religion that forced its members to understand religion as a recognition of this authority.

the history of christianity is no less a history with two lines running counter to each other, one line of pure doctrine and valid laws and one line of lived christianity, or better, a line that tried to live christianity. think of the history of monks and orders concerned with real christianity right into the middle ages, with a form of living christianity, not teaching it in the sense of a binding law or a binding theology. think of the reformation, although this then had the consequence of church and state joining in a new and closer alliance that made only official christianity possible. ultimately religion was so perverted that the prince had to determine the confession to which one belonged.

any move towards an ideology is paralysis. and the more a truth-protecting institution attempts to make truth institutional, down to death sentences, the more it is out of tune with the times. and the more it persecuted william of ockham, who had a few thoughts about papacy and the council, as an innovator and stuck to tradition, the more it was pushed into the cold of history.

if william of ockham designs a new philosophy that can replace the aristotelian tradition, there is little sense in making thomas aquinas a saint as an aristotelian to secure its own tradition. the new thinking, the via moderna, to which luther appealed, takes its course.

and so today there is a church that has to do without a large number of christian initiatives because they have developed outside institutionalized truth. the workers' movement, the emancipation of women, the peace movement, the anti-war movement are fundamentally christian approaches, but the church misses them because it has been forced into a conservative position. by this i mean the official church or official churches. this does not mean that there are not many christians who are aware of the roots of these movements and take initiatives within them, though certainly as expelled individuals. today christianity no longer belongs to the church, and has not done so for a long time.

the church had a priest called lamennais flung into prison because he, long before the great socialists, pointed out the christian motives of the workers' movement.

the church blessed the weapons of war and justified nuclear war, so long as it was a just war.

the pope once forbade modern architecture for churches when the whole of the world had shown itself open to modern ideas.

in some cases the church fell into line, but often it was behind the times and showed itself to be insensitive and uncreative. and this was not just on contemporary questions, but also on the principal topics of christianity. one need only look at the church's attitude to colonialism and the theology of liberation. as long as colonialism protected missionaries it was correct. a theology of liberation endangers the link between church and state, and thus the state that sustains it.

christianity went outside a long time ago. new testament religion does not have to wait for recognition from the established church in order to develop. even the said lamennais, once an opponent of the french revolution, spoke up for democracy and social commitment while the church was defending the monarchy as a gift from god. it took a hundred years to reach the position by which it can just save its face today.

this need not cause a lot of emotion today. that is justified by the structure of the thing. christianity is not the result of a reform of the temple-palace in jerusalem. christianity has gone elsewhere and will continue to go elsewhere for as long as it is perceived as doctrine and law.

there is still a great human force, a force for human persistence and survival in the fact that people turn to the poor, the little men and those who have been left behind. it does not matter how the rich industrial nations are reminded about the poor of the world. what matters is that the state of affairs itself be changed, not bringing an ideology into play.

a world without war, a technology of humane responsibility, education to be oneself, education free of the imposition of will from above, an earth without a preferred belief-authority, a humanity of sharing, these are all goals with a christian view of things, even if the copyright is now scarcely discernible. the sermon on the mount is still a source of fundamental human change, for the individual and the world.

the world has accepted more christian ideas than the church has preached. and the womb of christianity contains crucial stimuli for a world without domination that does not have to be identified by preachers. and as a rule they cannot do it, because they think in teaching categories, not in living categories.

and so even today there are still no christians who would also be republicans, apart from a few who are not even the famous exception that can be forgotten. democrats, yes there have been some of those recently. but who will speak up for the abolition of politics from above, who stands for the model of a state that comes from below? which christians today oppose the "christian state" that so far is still a state controlled from above?

but this does not help very much. whether official christianity takes part in some movement that follows fundamental christian ideas in fact matters very little. the church is as much in the cold as the religion-protecting high priests on mount zion. christ's teaching is nowhere preserved in an institution. it is lived, it is not previously there. and so it is lived by someone who understands it as a life form.

now this could all sound as though there does not need to be a church. that would be a misunderstanding. there are occasions on which church administrations can be useful, just like any other office. it is just that things can no longer be turned on their heads. it is not the post office that created letter writing, but vice versa, the post office is there because people write letters. we do not deny the fact that bureaucracies have become so powerful all over the world that, in order to remain in the picture, the post office would be in a position to abolish letter writing. it does not alter the fact that adminstrations, even religious ones, only have the minds of administrators.

it is a deeply ingrained mistake of christians to keep looking at something up there. christian existence is lived existence. anyone who thinks like this has the refreshing experience that alongside the church that is known to us there is a quite different church, the church of those who are known by their fruits. theology is generous with the allocation of churches. there is the mystical church, the church of the saints, and why should there not be another, the church of lived christianity?

if one looks at the world more closely, one discovers that its condition is dependent upon biographies. its condition is always determined by people, individual people made of flesh and blood, with obligations and desires. they themselves are the result of a life form. they are what they are not because they belong to a family, a party or a state. the more they represent their own life the more impressive they become. they do not have to be great, or have a name. their person is their identity.

this point of view allows us to discern what we call christianity. even if one is careful with allocations and classifications, people with a quite definite attitude will be discerned. they have a certain profile. they want different things from other people. and one finds how broad and deep christian behaviour is. one discovers what they do from the reason for which they do it.

sometimes it's a real christian, sometimes it isn't. sometimes it's a professor, sometimes an ordinary worker, sometimes it's an academic, sometimes it's someone with no profession at all. what he has made of his life is unmistakable. it has different motivation. it is strong as a result of involvement, care and helpful actions. and it can be recognized from something that today is seen almost as unrealistic: he does not think in terms of profits.

and yet it is not always easy to recognize fundamentally christian attitudes. today's christian is as a rule conformist, protects his religion like an ideology, pays attention to externals, arrangements for services, toeing the line, signs of membership, demonstrations of belonging. christian things are strong only in exceptions. otherwise they look like a political party in pursuit of belonging to a religion. christians are supporters trained in humility, for nietzsche despicable deniers of self, victims of constant indoctrination.

set against this is a person of a different selflessness, one not based on achievement, profit, success, honour and recognition, as appropriate to the modern image of the middle-class personality that is typical of today's world. the christian ethos is different. if it is selfless it is not to dedicate itself to an ideology, however just this may be. it is selfless without making any charge.

christians in galilee and the high priests in the temple believed in the same god of the fathers. and yet the former rebelled, because religion can degenerate into superficiality. they went another way. they left what was old to be. and this from a self-confidence that many would denounce as inimical to religion. they did it because they trusted themelves as well, and the way of their own that they were following.

cultures of thinking

in 1935 a young english mathematician studying in cambridge ran so far north of the town in the direction of ely on his cross-country runs that he could see the mighty cathedral there. he thought that he had reasons to make demands on his body that meant that he could keep a check on himself. on one of these runs he had an idea about how he could tackle a problem of mathematical logic that was bothering mathematicians ond logicians at the time. it is known that physical movement can stimulate thought, and a long run alone might create particularly favourable conditions for thinking unusual thoughts.

the problem was mathematics' freedom from contradiction, the question of whether its methods can be subjected to conclusive proof. this had been postulated by the german mathematician david hilbert of göttingen. his view was that "any well-defined mathematical question must of necessity have an exact solution."

the mathematician kurt gödel, born in Brno and the hungarian mathematician john von neumann, now both exiles in england, had succeeded in proving that hilbert was not right. mathematics cannot use mathematical methods to prove that its procedures are not ultimately open to contradiction. there is no logical way of presenting its results as conclusive. the best possibility was a real way of, as von neumann said, creating experimental proofs by "mechanical methods", in other words arriving at the truth by means of successful operations.

alan turing - this was the young cambridge mathematician - hit upon the idea of building a mathematical machine that can carry out such operations. this was the hour of the modern computer's birth. the proof lay in a machine that can carry out all mathematical processes in their most complex version. as an automatized and universal calculator it should be able to calculate endlessly without needing to present proofs.

it turned out that others, partly for different reasons, were on the same track, and it was not to be until after the war that turing and others were able to build a computer on the basis not of electrical technology, but the newly developed electronic technology.

at that time ludwig wittgenstein was going down another path in cambridge, revising his former views, and occasionally turing and wittgenstein found it possible to discuss their opposing stances.

the war required calculating machines, not just to work out trajectories and supply problems, but to decode enemy information and news. the new age was born, the age of electronics and digital precision. the calculating machines were a product of the war, but also a requirement of civilization.

the english had been able to halt the german manufacture of submarines, a rational-heroic expression of total war, by developing observation and calculation techniques that allowed them to locate the submarines and destroy them. scientists that hitler had driven out of the country played a considerable part in this. the german forces ran into the trap of the intelligence that hitler had driven out. the response to the mass production of submarines was in terms of calculating machines.

the times as a whole required a new, faster, more precise method of processing data and information. air traffic, the national economy, the movement of capital, even tourism needed more efficient methods of data transmission, to say nothing of processing data for science and research.

the computer had to be invented and it was also invented in several places, simply because the flood of information and the hunger for information could not have been handled in any other way.

but what happened as a result of this is the reciprocal process that society, economy and science adapted themselves to the computer and changed themselves into a structure that could be counted. the medium is the message. we are developing a culture and a civilization that are adapted to the computer, based upon deterministic regularity and allocating everything its place and its number.

in his dialogue with turing, wittgenstein was concerned to show that the world does not consist merely of quantities, but also of meanings. meanings are evaluations. our language as a vehicle for cognition and insight is never precise and consistent, every word changes according to usage and mis-usage, constantly acquires new evaluations. and an evaluation that includes personal, social and cultural factors is too complex to be handled in terms of mathematics. it can only be expressed in a judgement, a statement.

turing had built machines intended to work like a brain. but the brain is not an inferential organ for logical steps, but an organ of evaluation, referring to its own self, not to rules that can be made objective. evaluation, establishing meaning, is not calculation. love and hate cannot be calculated, and neither can functionality or aesthetic beauty.

the age belonged to turing and the other mathematicians like norbert wiener, john von neumann, claude shannon, who had developed "the thing", after the atomic bomb the second product of technology that was to put its stamp upon the century. but turing saw the computer less as a machine that did calculations - they were already there for simple arithmetic. he saw it as a machine of logical control, as a thought principle. for him the application of mathematics to logic, as for the wiener kreis, for example, followed the application of technology to logic.

the age belongs above all to the millions and millions of computers in banks, universities, factories, research institutions, offices and police stations. we will have to work on the basis that all the information that now needs to be processed makes it necessary to entrust ourselves even more to computerization than happens today.

and now we have to ask the question: is that the way things are going? to which incidentally no computer would know an answer.

this question is also being examined from another side, from the point of view of neurophysiology, brain research. here too different methods of data processing are emerging, a calculating one and an evaluating one. there is an analytical and a synthetic side to the brain, one that draws conclusions in the digital sense and one that looks in the analogous sense.

it is possible to throw oneself at computer development and work on computer science, computer art, computer politics, computer economics and computer medicine, as all representatives of the fashionable zeitgeist do. let us forget that, in spite of all the undisputed advantages that a computer brings as a useful tool.

in reality we are faced with a cultural dilemma: do we give ourselves over to the logical determinism of precise methods of calculation or do we burst the framework of a one-dimensional civilization of order and classification that is always one of subordination and dominance at the same time?

our culture is like its methodological trappings, like its technology. quantification and capitalization will increase with every computer that is installed. we count and calculate, commission others to count and calculate. this restricts all our freedoms, except that of arithmetical development. even the quality of a newspaper is now reduced to a struggle about higher circulation figures.

this is not about a revolt against the computer age. it is about proving that brain and thinking are much more complicated than can be represented in mathematical methods. a humane world will have to admit to itself that people think differently from computers. it is not the question of artificial intelligence that determines the quality of our culture, but the insight that computers cannot fall in love and do not even know what they would do with a picture by picasso. there are no computers calling for freedom. they calculate, but do not evaluate. they do not know what is significant. computers do not have the reference point that is significant for all human insight.

cognition is not being, but behaviour. nothing exists except in meaning. meaning is an individual, personal correspondence between me and my surroundings, in which i am, live and act.

the modern individual can be perceived as a craft moving in space, with no orientation point but other craft, which are also moving. the whole system revolves and turns, there is no fixed point of reference. this cosmos looks different from every flying point. each point has its own situation, its particular individuality.

people constantly change their positions, whether in terms of geography, profession, convictions or inclinations. points of reference are a set of moving surroundings with constantly changing faces and constantly new ideas, new positions.

the one fixed point of reference is the individual ego. this ego achieves an adjustment of the quality of a movement in a movement. this can only be mastered from an awareness of position. there is no co-ordination, or as much as you want. if there are several points in space then the question of distance, whether near or far, is different for every point. every point, every ego finds a new set of situations.

a computer is a cupboard, a box, a piece of standing equipment. its world can be reduced to a system of co-ordinates, to numbers and the operations that can be conducted with numbers. a computer has a fixed position. its world is static like the world of science, but also boundless. our world is limited, but dynamic. even turing had the impression that a perfect computer would have to learn to walk, to move.

there is another factor. our insights are a menu. we do not cook only with water or only with salt. one of the insights of refined cookery is that plenty of sugar should be added to anything salty.

the brain is constantly faced with a complex, moving situation when it is required to take us towards a decision. and the data it receives are differently structured. sweet and sour, solid and liquid come together. there is aesthetic information that cannot be captured in numbers and quantities. there are moral quantities. we think in pictures. nature secures its persistence and development in reproduction relating to love at first sight.

the interpersonal element in our life-cosmos rests largely upon aesthetic judgement, evaluation of visual data. we react to gestures, facial expressions, impressions. our culture is largely one of sensory perception. culture is the school of aesthetic judgement.

let us record the following facts:
1. human insights are those of movement in a moving system.
2. the reference point is the individual ego. the position of the system is established as soon as there is a fixed point. that is the particular individual.
3. for the individual everything that has meaning is significant. definition of the position is an evaluation.
4. there are various kinds of information. they cannot necessarily be referred to each other. there is information in dimensions and figures. there is information with compelling logical conclusions. there is aesthetic information. there are ethical evaluations.
5. the brain processes information as a menu.

thinking leading to logical conclusions is not the same as viewing-thinking. we can even be concretely aware of it. if we involve ourselves in thinking to draw logical conclusions we say that we have to concentrate. and here concentration means switching off all the thought-mechanisms that influence or can overlay linear logical thought. we admit only a certain form of thought, cut out other forms of thought and switch off the light of our brain's other functions. this is what we call concentration. but there are other forms of thought.

as a rule the brain operates like an orchestra with a large number of instruments. sometimes we like just one instrument to play. what is analogous and what is digital?

you have to cut a piece of paper in half. either you take a ruler, measure the page and halve the measurement. or you fold the paper and gently fix the crease. one procedure is analogous, the other digital. digital means working with figures, analogous means working with comparisons.

a digital clock gives only a numerical value, an analogous clock a position of the hands.

a woman wants to pick out her two longest knitting needles. she either measures them all, or she puts the whole bundle on the table and chooses the two that are longest. the digital process establishes quantities, the analogue shows quality, and this at the first attempt.

at siemens in munich they say that if you want a calculator the best thing to do is go across the road and buy one. applying for one from the firm, that does itself make calculators, takes too long. the company is too big, its management is digital. the board sees only figures: turnover, profit, yield.

the reputation of a state feeds on the names of its large concerns. but about 80 per cent of industrial products are made by middle-sized firms. middle-sized firms do not have big names, but they are efficient and flexible. they are managed on a basis of perception, looking at things, an overall view, in other words, by analogous means. they need no bureaucracy.

an experienced cook does not need a recipe book. he does not need figures for quantities and weights, he cooks from his own experience. what makes him a good cook is his taste, his tongue and his experience with controlling quality.

thomas jefferson thought up a state run from below, built on the democracy of local communities. democracy develops through the object with which it is concerned, and from perception, from the perception of interests as well. america has acquired a centralized state of orders and directives from above, and this is statistically orientated, in just the same way as the french revolution imagined a state based on reason. reason keeps to the general, not the particular, reason relies on drawing logical conclusions, not on perception.

logical thinking is an operation like a calculation. logical conclusions are drawn from premises. meanings degenerate to a status that is processed according to the operating rules. the end is a result. as in a calculation. logical thinking can think only one thought, and think it through.

analogous thinking refers to several things. comparisons can be made only between at least two things. comparisons provide insights, not results. judgements are made, but a logical conclusion is not reached. it is only full consideration that makes it possible to see entire landscapes.

we are in the middle of a comprehensive revolution that we scarcely perceive simply because it does not make any noise. we are leaving the parental home of our image of the world and going out into the open cosmos of self-determination. we are leaving the basis of our previous thought culture, our static view of the world as a jointed building of logic, precision and determined relationships. this existence was great and boundless. it was defined according to general and universal principles. it had cause and effect. the general was above the particular.

and now we are standing outside, we are ourselves responsible for what we do and make. it nearly gives us shock to see that the world is such as we make it. our cosmos is becoming narrower but more complex. our thinking needs other tools, another principle. precise methods are little use to us when the instruments no longer grip. we live in uncertain relationships. we have to commit ourselves to assessing the position, to our own point of view, to evaluating and allotting meanings. data can be investigated by our own intervention and our own design, the great starry sky above has weakened in the haze of the cities.

we no longer find a guiding spirit for the world, and we have liberated ourselves from accommodating to the laws of such a spirit. the world is the one that we have furnished for ourselves. as it is in a questionable condition, represents a critical mass, we have to see whether we will not merely have to learn to take responsibility for it, but beyond that to develop methods of design that open up better perspectives. even philosophy must become an activity. an activity involved with clearing up the everyday.

perhaps immanuel kant is at the beginning of this movement. at first he thought he had completed his work with the *critique of pure reason* and the *critique of practical reason.* he had shown that cognition was based on synthetic sentences a priori, in which, as in mathematics, abstract categories are linked. truth is conceptuality free of contradiction. but he does accept that it presupposes a view of things, and experience.

then kant finds a new subject for philosophy. man is concerned not only with truth, but also with expediency. expediency becomes the new criterion for truth. and the power of cognition directed at expediency has other bases for evaluation than such powers based on truth. it does not derive from logical conclusions but from reflective, evaluating judgements. it derives from subjective statements and submits the world to teleological evaluation. he calls the organ of this evaluation "reflective judgement", in contrast with determining understanding, which reaches its conclusions "mechanically".

the world is viewed in terms of its fulfilment of purpose, no longer its causality. there is finality. "everything in the world is good for something. nothing in it is in vain." But is is not now logical finality, but actual finality.

"reflective judgement" is assisted by "imagination". unlike reason, it is not applied to the general, but to the particular.

later, for darwin, development no longer had a final goal. everything that exists is a result of trial and error under the qualification criteria of efficiency, the survival of the fittest. but kant takes a decisive step from the determinist philosophy of logical necessity into a reflective evaluation of expediencies that are always survival chances as well. kant is already aware that "nature organizes itself . . . as itself, and yet provides all manner of seemly deviations required for survival according to the circumstances". he sees analysis of purposes as "one more principle" for which the laws of causality are inadequate.

then later wittgenstein says: we must go back from reasons to descriptions. finally wittgenstein, as a former purist of precise method went as far as to question whether humanity, with "its scientific cognition" is not "running into a trap" that "is the beginning of the end".

our understanding is to see our thinking as innate, as a natural condition. in reality our thinking is a product of education and culture.

precise science, precise technology have taken us into the farthest galaxies. we are acquiring a picture of the origin of the universe, from a zero point that was also the origin of time and space.

the equivalent of this flight into infinity is failure in the finite, the final balance is negative. the intellectual edifice of precise reason and the harvest of regulated knowledge are large and broad. here on the planet we are anxious about survival. we have denied the very thing that supports our existence for too long.

we have allowed ourselves to be intoxicated by a world dominated by figures and quantities, and have lost sight of the cosmos of values, of meanings.

with exact science, with computerized technology we can run from success to success towards the end of the world. the prospects of our doing it are recognizable. we should need another way of thinking. this would not necessarily be defined by different aims. we need different methods, different points of view, different procedures. the human mind has too long been a plaything of the intellectual glass bead game of exact methods.

we do not know whether telescopes will still be looking out into space in a hundred years. the age of pure abstraction no longer offers secure prospects.

we are now brought up as cultural beings that think and consume. the world frame by which we orientate ourselves is one of exact results. reason drawing logical conclusions used to be our orientation method. now calculating automata have risen to be the intelligence that guides us.

at the same time we have become incapable of doing anything. we are involved in the world as a result of opinions, not interventions, actions and designs. we go to vote every four years and fit in with the numbers produced by this. in fact we decide in terms of what will ensure consumption.

modern man as a product of his culture is a thinking and consuming being. his ability to make anything, his ability to design anything is atrophying. he is becoming passive, and his activities are going into decline. the machine to which we entrust our thinking demands that we act according to the image of the machine.

we can all see the condition of this world. we all know that something should be done. but all we produce is appeals. we are fully and consciously engaged in a process the end of which is foreseeable, but there is a danger that there is nothing more that we can do. we have become children of a thought culture that has disconnected thinking from making, so that it can be locked on to logical precision alone. doing has been replaced by the pleasures of consumption.

we are in the prison of our own reason. the more we know, the less we can do.

afterword

the first aircraft driven by the power of human muscles, the first flying machines as artefacts of man himself, were built in sheds on the edge of los angeles. mc cready thinks that they could never have been created in the laboratories of large-scale industry because the thought culture of largescale industry would have been unsuitable for them. the experience upon which such industry built up its successes would have been too narrow a basis.

turing's machines as well, the first computers, were not produced in IBM or Bell laboratories, but in sheds and shacks in the country, usually with just one technical assistant. it was only industrial exploitation that took place in academic institutions or large-scale industrial laboratories.

the results of large-scale operations are like the operations themselves. the result is appropriate to the method.

i mention this simply to justify methods that lie outside traditional organizational forms and have no public blessing.

most of the essays in this volume were written in the last twelve years. their basic positions go back to the fifties, to the time when the author was a co-founder of the hochschule für gestaltung in ulm, and taught there.

the texts address the philosophical bases of design and architecture, the interconnection of sensory perception and thought, the role of physical experience and manual intelligence and philosophies that made important contributions to these subject areas.

the essays were written within an unpretentious institution called the "institute for analogous studies". it is a workshop for study, not for proclamations. these essays were based on discussion, practical experience, case observations, model experiments. and this in a very untidy, disorganized, unsystematic way. there was no budget, no director, just the topic.

this institution is within some graphic design studios, within visual designs, which inevitably led to emphasis being placed on practical experience. in the graphic arts as well a great deal of emphasis is placed on getting away from mathematics, in which graphics had become involved through the influence of movements like concrete art. understanding visual language as communication means leaving the spell of precise, syntactical rule-games and turning to communicative performance, to the kind of communication that it has to offer.

significant attempts were made to set up a visual encyclopaedia of the world, but unfortunately insufficient record was kept of such model experiments.

despite all this, several essays were produced. some of them were offered for public evaluation in lectures and publications. no applications were made for support from the public purse, and no such applications should be made.

sources

"grasping with the hand and mind", in *greifen und griffe*, cologne 1987.

"extensions of the ego", in *greifen und griffe*, cologne 1987.

"the eye, visual thinking", lecture to the medical faculty of the university of essen, 1988.

"analogous and digital", *circular*, 1, 1978.

"universals and capitals", in *in rotis*, no place, 1987.

"architecture and epistemology" in *norman foster. buildings and projects of foster associates*, volume 2, berlin 1989.

"planning and control", *arch+*, no. 18 (april 1989).

"life form and ideology", in *löscht den geist nicht aus. festschrift für norbert greinacher*, munich 1991.